Dr. Samuel L. Banks Speaks

"Selected Writings"
1990-1995

Edited by

Collis Delano Patterson

authorHOUSE®

AuthorHouse™
1663 Liberty Drive
Bloomington, IN 47403
www.authorhouse.com
Phone: 833-262-8899

Published by AuthorHouse 10/01/2025

ISBN: 978-1-4389-2489-2 (sc)
ISBN: 978-1-4389-2488-5 (hc)
ISBN: 978-1-4670-4809-5 (e)

Library of Congress Control Number: 2008910494

Print information available on the last page.

This book is printed on acid-free paper.

CONTENTS

Introduction

I met Dr. Samuel L. Banks in 1973 when he was Coordinator of Social Studies for the Baltimore City Public Schools. He impressed me as a very caring, intelligent, and dedicated man.

As our friendship developed, he became my mentor and advisor. When I began my career as a teacher, Dr. Banks was very supportive of my philosophy and ideas regarding education and African American students.

Dr. Banks wrote a book regarding the education of black children and youth which inspired me and many other teachers to continue my efforts to teach African American children. Dr. Banks motivated many people in many ways, but I think his most important means of influence was through his writings. He wrote about subjects ranging from Affirmative Action to the confirmation of Supreme Court Justice Clarence Thomas. Dr. Banks was a master of words; indeed, it was not uncommon for him to create his own words. All of his writings teach lessons and one can learn a lot from them.

I often wondered why Dr. Banks sent me all of his writings. Perhaps it was because he felt they would help me develop own my writing skills. He probably also believed I would publish these writings for the world to read. I want Dr. Banks and his legacy to live forever; this book is the best to do this. Dr. Samuel L. Banks touched the lives of people of all races. Those of us who knew him personally during the time that he was on this earth were blessed and fortunate to have been in his presence.

When Dr. Banks passed away in July of 1995, I was at Ohio State University studying Arabic culture and language. I wrote this poem to my dear friend and cherished mentor, Dr. Samuel L. Banks.

Passing

Unless you suffer, and dip your pen into the very depth of your sorrow, your rhymes will remain mere glittering ornaments, dry bones in a marble tomb.

Wonderful Times, Bad Times. Is this not the trial of passing through the world? Suffering, living a living hell, a living hell.

There is a door that you pass through first, and one that you pass through last.

Living, lying, loving, and hoping. It is time to go. Don't hurry, don't hurry, and don't hurry, because one door you pass though first and one that you pass through last.

Listening, laughing, leaving and coping. There is nothing to do, there is nothing to do. Overtax your body; overtax your mind, even your spirit. It makes no difference because when you pass though the door, the first one you pass through then you pass though the last.

Rest, rest, wait, wait, love, live, hope, cope, laugh, leave, suffer and maybe you will pass though the pearly gates and sit beside Him and be with Him.

Collis D. Paterson

Acknowledgements

I would first like to thank the members of the Baltimore Branch of the Association for the Study of Afro American Life and History for encouraging me to publish this book. Thanks are also due to Dr. Cynthia Neverdon-Morton, who inspired me to persist in this project after encouraging me to write an article in the Negro History Bulletin.

Many thanks to Jennifer D. Gibson for typing and editing the manuscript and to Dr. Jacqueline Frierson for writing the epilogue.

Thanks to Allegro Communications, Inc. for designing the cover, to the Black Caucus for contributing toward the expenses of completing the book, to and to Jennifer Rucker for the final editing of the book. Cheryl Coates of Black Classic Press, Inc. and Alice Cherbonnier of Allegro provided valuable advice on printing and publishing. Special thanks to Willis lee B. Jones for his help.

Dedication

This book is dedicated to the memory of Dr. Samuel L. Banks, and to his family.

Dr. Samuel L. Banks
Administrator, Teacher, Author, Professor, Advocate, Consultant and Humanitarian

"The risk of hope needs to be taken now in support of our nation's greatest and most valuable investment-all of its children and you!"

The death of Dr. Samuel L. Banks leaves a deep void in the Baltimore City Public Schools. Dr. Banks served as the Director of the Department of Compensatory Education and Funded Programs and was widely known throughout the nation for his leadership in Afrocentric education and curriculum reform as well as for his writings. In recognition of his leadership in history and the social sciences, he was appointed to the National Commission of History Standards.

Dr. Banks received his B.A. from Howard University in history and political science. He earned a doctorate in educational administration with high distinction from George Washington University. He also engaged in post-doctoral study at Harvard University as a Fellow of the National Endowment for the Humanities.

Dr. Banks wrote *Stony the Road: The Black American, in the American Experience* (1972), *The Education of Black Children and Youths; A Framework for Excellence* (1985). He was a contributor to Crime in the Black Community (1976) and was working on his third book at the time of his death, with James Jackson Kilpatrick: *School Desegregation in Virginia, 1952-1964*. His other publications include over 75 articles germane to education, contemporary issues and Afrocentric education.

Dr. Banks' professional and community affiliations include: Phi Delta Kappa Honor Fraternity, Tau Kappa Pi Honor Society, Who's Who in School Districts, and teacher and member of the Board of Deacons of the Walker Memorial Baptist Church. Dr. Banks was also adjunct professor of education at Morgan State University. He received the Maryland Region, National Conference of Christians and Jews Human Relations Award in education, and received the Baltimore Branch of the Association for Study of Afro-American

History's "Conservator of Carter G. Woodson Legacy Award. Dr. Banks was past national president of the Association for the Study of Afro-American Life and History. On June 27, 1993, Dr. Banks was commencement speaker at So-journer-Douglass College. His many other honors included the Governor's Citation for Professional Leadership and the Mayor's Citation for Professional Contributions.

On February 23, 1997 the Baltimore City Public Schools renamed and dedicated its Professional Development Center in honor of the many accomplishments of *Dr. Banks the Dr. Samuel L. Banks Professional Development Center.*

Dr. Banks directed and implemented the first multi-ethnic/multi-racial social studies program for kindergarten to twelfth grade from 1970 to 1972, which earned him national acknowledgement. This curriculum became a part of the National Educational Retrieval Information Center.

He was also a popular newspaper writer in Baltimore, Washington, D.C. and Norfolk. He wrote articles for the *Baltimore Afro-American, The Baltimore Times, The Washington Afro-American*, and the *Norfolk Journal and Guide.*

In his leisure time, Dr. Banks enjoyed reading, swimming and stamp collecting.

A native of Norfolk, Virginia. Dr. Banks was married to the former Elizabeth Harvey. The couple had two daughters, Gayle Bernette Banks Jones and Allison Faith Banks Holmes, and had three granddaughters Nicole, Elizabeth and Brittany Jennelle Jones. Dr. Banks died in July of 1995.

1990

Pratt's Victory in Washington Has Profound National Importance

The political reverberations of Sharon Pratt Dixon's historic and resounding victory in Washington, B.C. have profound and far-reaching implications for our nation. Mrs. Dixon, through her extraordinary triumph as D.C.'s new mayor, has demonstrated convincingly, palpably and inspirationally that where a fair, just, and equal environment exists, merit, unusual ability, and hard work will prevail. Tragically, far too often in the American political, economic, and educational arenas, the elemental elements of simple justice, equality of opportunity and fair play have not been in place for Black citizens, Hispanics, Native Americans, women and the poor. Bountiful and heartfelt felicitations to mayor-elect Sharon Pratt Dixon on her marvelous victory and forging a new political course in Washington, D.C.

There are two other salient and valuable lessons to be learned from Mrs. Dixon's overwhelming victory over Maurice Turner, former D.C. Chief of Police and the Republican standard-bearer. In this conjunction, it is interesting to observe that last spring when polls were being taken, there was almost a universal belief that Mrs. Dixon would not be a serious candidate because of the lack of name recognition, inadequate funding for her campaign and allegations that she would be a "tool" of the D.C. corporate community. In point of fact, the front-runners were identified often in the media, print and electronic, as Councilman John Ray, Councilwoman Charlene Drew Jarvis, Council President David Clarke, and D.C. Delegate Walter Fauntroy. Sharon Pratt Dixon was considered a distant fifth. However, her tenacity, drive, fertile and trenchant mind, outstanding educational preparation and superb speaking ability enabled her, especially after she received media attention, the necessary margin for her to be highly effective and decisive in the primary and general elections. There can be no repressing of outstanding ability, intrepidity and rugged determination when the playing field is level and equality of opportunity, in fact, exists.

Mrs. Dixon's victory provides concrete and incontestable evidence to Black America, in particular, that strong, solid, and splendid academic preparation, resiliency, excellent organizational and research skills, fierce pride in self and in ones historical roots and a willingness to take the proverbial leap of faith, even in the face of institutional racism and exclusion from the socio-economic mainstream, when equal opportunity and social justice prevail, can enable one to our to the heights.

At a time when 250 million Americans are reeling from President George Bush's repudiation of the Civil Rights Act of 1990 passed by overwhelming majorities of the House and Senate, and a pervasive sense exists that the nation has begun a retreat on human and civil rights, the remarkable victories of Sharon Pratt Dixon, Eleanor Holmes Norton, Rev. Jesse Jackson, among others in D.C., and Alexander Williams as Prince George's State's Attorney, show that we need not despair, but dare to push forward for our full manhood-womanhood rights throughout the United States. Young Black Americans who, even at this late date, have failed to see the nexus or connection between education and the political process and workplace should be encouraged by Black political successes, in the face of fearsome adversities and obstacles, and get serious about education and vertical mobility.

David Dinkins, Mayor of New York, Coleman Young, Mayor of Detroit, and a host of other Black politicos provide steadying and heartening evidence that education, hard work, imaginativeness and willingness to be a risk taker, where genuine equality of opportunity is in place, will make an important difference.

Finally, Sharon Pratt Dixon's success in Washington, D.C. signals afresh that the old order, in reality, has changed and a new day beckons. Mayor Marion S. Barry, Mrs. Dixon's predecessor, now passes from D.C.'s political scene having failed in his bid to win an at-large D.C. Council seat. Nonetheless, even in defeat at in the council manic race, Barry received over 50,000 votes.

However, the D.C. electorate determined in its collective wisdom and sophistication that Mesdames Linda Crop and Hilda Mason were better choices. The Barry era passes; Sharon Pratt Dixon's begins suspiciously. The voters of Washington, D.C after enduring over five years of political trauma, pain, and disillusionment associated with the Barry investigation and conviction, have demonstrated sagacity, prudence, flexibility, fairness, and amazing grace under pressure. Their collective example, in this instance, can serve as a national model of how the political process should work.

Christmas 1990

The boundless joy, rich expectancy and enveloping vibrancy and euphoria, associated with Christmas, although fleeting, provide a universal uplift and inspiration for disparate socio-racial and religious groups throughout the world.

The world community is affected very positively by an infectious spirit of fellow-feeling and togetherness, concern for others, especially the poor and excluded, and a timeless resolve to celebrate, in special and magnanimous ways, the extra-ordinary birth of Jesus Christ in Bethlehem over 2,000 year ago.

In this wondrous sense, men and women of decency and good will, in earnest, can lustily proclaim: "Joy to the world, the Lord is come, let earth proclaim His name."

As we observe Christmas this year, amidst our personal happiness and gratitude, we must understand that in a large sense the Christmas season exemplifies the "Best of times and the worst of times."

While we may rejoice at this time, there, too, is the sobering and disquieting reality that there are too many instances of human suffering and conflict throughout the world. The situation is especially bleak for a disproportionate number of Black Americans, Hispanics, Native Americans and the impoverished. Amoral imperative exists for all of us, in our distinctive ways, to brighten the corner where we are.

The socio-economic condition of over one-third of Black Americans or two million Black citizens is grim, painful and troubling.

The decision of George Herbert Walker Bush, abandoning his call for a "kinder, gentler America," to veto the Kennedy-Hawkins Civil Rights Act of 1990 has been a crushing and psychologically numbing blow for 35 million Black Americans irrespective of socio-economic standing or academic-intellectual attainments.

President Bush by his decision to veto the Civil Rights Act of 1990 has the Ignoble and ignominious distinction of becoming the third president of our new nation's history to veto a civil rights bill.

The two former presidents to repudiate civil rights bills were Andrew .Johnson and Ronald Wilson Reagan.

What really hurts Black Americans insofar as President Bush's rejection of the Civil Rights Act was the failure of the President to be truthful and forthright about the contents of the civil rights legislation?

It was patently wrong, illogical and unfair for President Bush to state that he vetoed the Civil Rights Act of 1990 because it provided for "quotas."

A bipartisan effort on the part of the Congress made certain that "quotas" would not be a part of the legislation. Equally important, the Civil Rights Act of 1990 was ratified by overwhelming majorities of the U.S. House and Senate.

The exhilaration, thankfulness and merriment associated with the Christmas season for Black Americans is dampened when they see their sons and daughters and loved ones involved in the military buildup in Saudi Arabia and the Persian Gulf and, simultaneously, experience the travail, pain and profound disappointment of President Bush rejecting the Civil Rights Act of 1990.

It is highly significant that Black persons constitute 30 percent of the U.S. military and that 20 percent of the military currently in Saudi Arabia and the Persian Gulf happen to be Black military personnel. We represent 12 per cent of our nation's population of 250 million citizens.

The recession or downturn in our economy is also wreaking havoc, unevenly, on Black citizens, Hispanics. Native Americans and the poor. Broad pockets of Black citizens in large urban areas are not experiencing a recession but economic depression of longstanding.

Our nation, even as it pours in one billion dollars a month for our military in Saudi Arabia and the Persian Gulf, must mobilize the will and human and monetary resources to address urgent human and social needs at home.

In spite of all of the adversities, vicissitudes, frustrations and deprivations in of the present, I urge you to continue, in season and out, to affirm hope human possibilities.

Troubles, to be sure, are not new to us as a people. I challenge you, this happy and enchanting season, to take the leap of faith and, above all, not to "weary of well-doing."

1991

Time for Jubilee in 1991

The past year has been a period of intense and painful vicissitudes, travail and disappointment for us as Black citizens.

Nonetheless, as in time past, we continue, thirty-five (35) million strong Black Americans, to inch forward and upward.

As we face the trials, challenges, uncertainties and opportunities in 1991, it is imperative that we redouble our efforts for social justice, economic parity, demonstrable excellence and collective survival and progress.

In spite of the resurgence of overt, operational and institutional racism and societal exclusion, we must resolve, through concrete actions, to have untrammeled freedom and equality of opportunity in the land of our birth.

The principle of full freedom and socio-economic equality must be made clear to the majority White society as a nonnegotiable issue in the "land of the free and the home of the brave."

We shall not permit our nation to deny our fundamental rights and socio-economic and educational equity and fairness.

In support of the ongoing struggle for human and civil rights for Black citizens, Hispanics, Native Americans and the poor, the celebration of the spirit and promise of Jubilee Day represents a marvelous way to begin 1991.

Jubilee Day, historically, has called attention to the official implementation of Abraham Lincoln's Emancipation Proclamation, which went into effect on January 1, 1863.

Lincoln had made clear to the Confederate states after the success of Union troops at the battle of Antietam in September, 1862 that all slavery would be abolished in Confederate states which remained in a state of rebellion after January 1, 1863.

While the Emancipation Proclamation did not, in fact, free slaves in the Confederacy, since the Union was not in control, it provided a powerful and compelling moral and ethical dimension to the Civil War.

Today, Jubilee Day is celebrated by the NAACP and Prince Hall Masons throughout the United States to celebrate and honor the promise and high human possibilities of the Emancipation Proclamation when it was announced to the world.

Two years later, in 1865, the heinous, depraved and reprehensible system of slavery was abolished by the adoption of the Thirteenth Amendment.

A categorical imperative exists, in spite of present disappointments, socio-economic barriers and a widening resistance to human and civil rights, for us us Black citizens to lend our unrelenting and unqualified support of Jubilee Day observances wherever we are located in our nation.

I offer a simple prescription as we launch into the deep of 1991: Get serious and get moving for our collective solidarity, pride and progress.

Dr. Martin Luther King, Jr. Remembered: Reviving The Fractured Dream

It is highly significant that the East Oliver Community Association, in concert with the solid and unwavering support of thirty-five (35) million fellow-Black Americans, in spite of the vicious, negative and mean-spirited efforts currently afoot to discredit and impugn Dr. Martin Luther King, Jr., the "apostle of non-violence and freedom" from Atlanta, Georgia, has decided to stand firmly, confidently and unashamedly behind him. Dr. King's contributions to our nation and the world are indelible, imperishable and towering. He is, beyond a doubt, a theologian and minister-educator extraordinaire. Dr. King is most worthy and deserving of our profound and abundant admiration and exultation.

BACKGROUND

In the historic "March on Washington" on Wednesday, August 28, 1963, I was exhilarated and inspired, as were over 250,000 fellow-citizens of our nation, Black and White, Hispanics, Asians and Native Americans, as Dr. King proclaimed, in part, in his immortal "I Have A Dream" oration: *It is obvious today that America has defaulted on this promissory note (i.e., concept of full freedom) insofar as her citizens of color are concerned. Instead of honoring this sacred obligation, America has given the Negro people a bad check; a check which has come back marked "insufficient funds." But we refuse to believe that the bank of injustice is bankrupt. We refuse to believe that there are insufficient funds in the grand vaults of opportunity of this nation. So we have come to cash this check-a check that will give us upon demand the riches of freedom and the security of justice. (1)*

Dr. King would continue:

We have come to this hallowed spot to remind America of the fierce urgency of *now*. This is no time to engage in the luxury of gradualism. Now is the time to make real the promises of democracy. *Now* is the time to open the doors of opportunity to all of God's children. *Now* is the time to lift our nation from the quick sands of racial injustice to the solid rock of brotherhood. (2)

I strongly believe, were Dr. King alive, he would still be about the serious and necessary business of social justice and equality of opportunity for all. The lamentable realities, even as we meet this evening in the auditorium of the proud Dr. Bernard Harris, Sr. Elementary School, that the political, socio-economic and educational situation has worsened for Black citizens, Hispanics, Native Americans and the poor. The social economic and educational condition is particularly grave and debilitating for Black citizens who have historically, boon excluded from the mainstream of American life. The grim statistical profile as it relates to Black citizens is well-known: unemployment among Black males hovers around 14 percent and 34 percent for Black youths during a time of unprecedented national prosperity; the Black student dropout-push out rate in 22 of 25 of the nation's predominantly Black school districts is close to 50 percent: 42.7 percent of Black children and youths under 18 are in a state of poverty; one-third of our about 12 million of the 35 million Black citizens in our nation are in poverty and identified by economists, politicians and sociologists as a tragic and unprofitable "permanent underclass." Black citizens are disproportionately represented in our nation's penal institutions, are housed in unsanitary, unsafe housing, and are the recipients of grossly inadequate health care We, too, suffer unevenly in terms of teenage pregnancies, substance abuse, AIDS and other medical disorders flowing essentially from poverty, poor education ,and institutional racism and societal exclusion. In spite of these painful and lugubrious circumstances, we must dare, as we pressure government at all levels (i e, local, state, federal) for legitimate support, to *DO MORE TO HELP OURSELVES*. We must not allow ourselves, notwithstanding the lack of equal opportunity and socio-economic justice, to become perpetual winners, complainers and mendicants.

As you full well know, when Dr King launched the Montgomery Bus Boycott under the banner of the Montgomery Improvement Association in December, 1955 there were many nay-Sayers and persons who believed that segregation the Montgomery buses could not be removed. Yet, amidst the chorus of denunciation, defiance, and resistance, Dr. King, incorporating with the unsung Black heroes and heroines who risked their jobs and lives to walk rather Hi in accept the humility and rank injustice of segregated buses, was able to provide intrepid, creative and persistent leadership which toppled segregated buses in Montgomery in 381 days.

The Challenge Of Dr. King's Rich Legacy For Us

Dr. King, to the very end, witnessed for full freedom and justice for all persons without fear or favor. His assassination on April 4, 1968 on the balcony of the Lorraine Motel in Memphis, Tennessee could not dissuade, impede or stop the grand and noble process he had begun for a just, equal and caring society. It now falls on each of us to become a part of the human process for creative tension and risk-takers for a better social order for all. I suggest, for you who are truly committed to positive change and, in fact, an egalitarian society, the following action-oriented elements:

1. Strike a blow for freedom, in honor of Dr. King. If you are not registered to vote, "REGISTER AND VOTE." Don't go fishing on Election Day if there is rain or other inclement circumstance.

2. Insist on demonstrable excellence in the schools in your community whether you have children in the schools or not. Make sure, through your direct involvement and participation with principals, teachers and central office support staff, on high expectations and optimum achievement for all children. In brief, work in full partnership with the schools.

3. Insist on school administrators who are able to articulate with clarity, confidence and force a vision of where the schools should be headed and who demonstrate, through concrete deeds and a clear "track record" that they are able to mobilize educators, parents, the corporate community, civic and political officials and students in showing that they can be forceful, fair and imaginative advocates for change and excellence.

4. Take an active role in political affairs. *Elected officials must be held accountable and responsible for their decisions.* Make sure that your elected officials reflect your interests and aspirations in the decision-making process. If not, you should actively seek and support others to represent your interests.

5. Work in vigorous and ongoing partnership with churches, civic groups, fraternities and sororities and elected officials to deter and eliminate escalating teenage pregnancies, drop-out/push-out levels in schools, rampant substance abuse and senseless and violent criminal activity that plague Black citizens. We must cease waiting for a secular savior to address problems within our immediate sphere of concerns.

6. Support and encourage Black entrepreneurial activity. Our use of the $260 billion part of the GNP must be more prudent and judicious.

7. As we read White dailies, we must become more supportive of Black newspapers, such as the *Amsterdam News*, the *Philadelphia Tribune*, the *Baltimore Afro-American*, the *Norfolk Journal and Guide,* the *Chicago Defender* and others. Our universal support of splendid Black-owned publications, such as Ebony and Jet, demonstrates that we can produce economic winners.

8. Become a risk-taker, wherever you are, for a more inclusive, open and just society. In other words, become less passive and more active for substantive and progressive change.

9. Become knowledgeable about and support Afro-centric and multiethnic-racial education in public schools. The emphasis must not be on supplanting European history, but on an inclusive and factual portrayal of American and world history which depicts the multidimensional as¬pects of Black life and history.

10. Take the time, if you have not done so, to read at least two books germane to Dr, King or Black life and history as we prepare to observe Black History Month in February, in addition to Dr. King's, *Stride Toward Freedom* and *Why We Can't Wait.*

11. We must be vigilant, active and insistent that the local and national media print and electronic portray Black citizens in a fair, accurate and comprehensive manner. Too much emphasis, at present, is on an invidious, stereotypical and negative portrayal of Black citizens. We must, through letters and calls to editors, managing editors and the Federal Communications Commission, insist on fairness, equity and justice in the media.

12. We must continue to support the NAACP, the Urban League, and SCLC, the 26-member Congressional Black Caucus, PUSH and other organizational efforts in support of an inclusive body political and human and civil rights. While we have made impressive societal gains as people in a subordinate and unequal status, we still have a mighty long way to go in order to achieve socio-economic educational and political parity.

Dr. Ben Carson's *Gifted Hands*, John Hope Franklin's, *From Slavery to Freedom* (sixth edition), Benjamin Quarles' *The Negro in the Making of*

America, John Johnson's *Succeeding Against the Odds*, and James Comer's *School Power* and Maggie's *American Dream* are highly recommended.

SUMMARY

We must continue, in spite of the trials and tribulations and privations of the present, to keep Dr. King's dream alive and dare, through it all, to push forward and upward. The times, to be sure, are difficult for us as Black citizens. We are still reeling, even as President George Herbert Walker Bush speaks of a "gentler and quieter America," from the President's repudiation of the Civil Rights Act of 1990 even after an overwhelming approval of the legislation by both the House and Senate of the United States Congress. We witness, too, a concerted and systematic attack on the principle of affirmative action and attenuated support for predominantly Black public schools and the 117 historically Black institutions of higher education. We witness, additionally, an upsurge in the pronouncements of hate, violence and divisiveness of such groups as the Ku Klux Klan and "Skinheads." In essence, as we observe Dr. King's sixty-second birthday, there is a discernible mood of retreat and re¬sistance to human and civil rights.

At present we are poised for a possible war in the Middle East because of the military aggression of Saddam Hussein of Iraq. Whether the supreme tragedy of war occurs in the Middle East, Black military personnel, numbering over 20 percent of the 400,000 troops and over 30 per cent of the U.S. Army of our nation, will be directly involved, as has been the case with us as Black citizens in every war in which our nation has participated. However, President Bush, through his feckless and indefensible veto of the Civil Rights Act of 1990, has put the human and civil rights of Black military personnel and 35 million Black citizens on hold.

As a people, in Dr. King's glorious memory, we must dare to uphold his dream and insist that our nation live up to its historic creed of "liberty and justice for all." A concluding word from Dr. King:

> *"I have a dream that one day every valley shall be exalted, every hill and mountain shall be made low, the rough places will be made plains, and the crooked places will be made straight, and the glory of the Lord shall be revealed, and all flesh shall see it together."*

It is in this marvelous and wondrous sense that I say to all of you gathered here this evening, let us, as a remarkable people who made the courageous and magnificent leap from slavery to freedom, dare to hold up, emulate and implement Dr. King's universal and impregnable dream. Hold your heads high as a proud and tested Watu Wazuri (i.e. Beautiful People) to keep the "Dream" alive.

The Baltimore Sunday Sun - February 17, 1991

Keep the Sanctions

Editor: The decision of President Frederick de Klerk of South Africa to eliminate the heinous and repugnant Group Areas Act, the Land Act, and Population Registration Act represents an important first step in ending the racial bifurcation and hostility between black and white South Africans. However, important as an extirpation of these oppressive measures is. It is not now a time for jubilation by South Africa's majority Black population or within the free world community.

President de Klerk and the South African parliament must now move with celerity and directness in granting the majority Black South African population a priceless and necessary right: the right of the ballot. Neither Nelson Mandela nor more than 25 million Black South Africans, in their native land, can enjoy the fundamental right of the vote. Moreover, political exiles are still denied the right to return home, the emergency detention laws which provide for indeterminate detention remain in effect and, above all, there is an abysmal absence of good-faith negotiations to accord the Black South African population socio-economic, educational and political parity.

Until there is substantive movement and decisive action on these issues, peace, tranquility and national unity will continue to elude South Africa. In the interim, I believe international sanctions against South Africa should remain in place.

Presented to the Forum Series of the Division of Instruction,
Baltimore City Public Schools March 21, 1991

An Afro Centric Curriculum: Strategies and Content

INTRODUCTION

The history of public education in our nation since its rudimentary beginnings in Massachusetts in the seventeenth century has largely reflected a Eurocentric or White portrayal of American and World History. Black and non-aim o people have been depicted, for the most part, in a tertiary, invidious and shoddy manner.

The upheavals in the 1960's which racked our nation, most notably in the large metropolitan areas, were directed toward correcting a virulent and pervasive racism and institutional subordination which afflicted our nation, past .mil present, but too, toward, an assiduous and concentrated effort to make elementary-secondary schools and institutions of higher education address the rich and variegated history of Black and non-white Americans. The persistent and unrelenting efforts for pertinence and "relevance" in elementary-secondary schools and institutions of higher education brought about tip-toeing and glacial change in terms of courses in Black History and multi-ethnic/ multicultural education.

The time, I believe, is now at hand when a substantive, in depth and factual portrayal is required of the rich, diverse, and remarkable contributions which Black Americans have made to American and world history in spite of formidable adversities. It is not the purpose of this brief paper, in view of a very limited time constraint, to develop a comprehensive analysis and synthesis of Black History, but to indicate, in a brief overview, what are the major components of Afrocentric programs. In this conjunction, two major points need to be fully understood in regard to how the larger white society, as a collective croup, past and present, views Black Americans:

1. NAGGING, PERSISTENT, AND HISTORIC QUESTIONS STILL REMAIN IN THE LARGER WHITE SOCIETY RELATIVE TO

THE FUNDAMENTAL HUMANNESS OR HUMANITY OF BLACK AMERICANS.

2. THE CONSTANT SOCIETAL PERCEPTION AND BELIEF REMAIN IN THE MAJORITY OF WHITE SOCIETY AS TO THE LEVEL OF EDUCABILITY OF BLACK CHILDREN AND YOUTHS.

While these two points, to be sure, are unsettling, vexatious and a source of incredulity for Black Americans, it is imperative that we meet these two colossal mythologies about us head-on through the force of truth and palpable deeds. Afrocentric education must accentuate our factual record, racial pride and validity, and determination to participate as full partners in the American social order.

ESSENTIAL COMPONENTS OF AN AFROCENTRIC HISTORY PROGRAM

I believe the following instructional elements or content should be encompassed in an Afrocentric program:

I. Africa before the Europeans Significant Ancient African Civilizations
II. Significant Ancient African Civilizations
A .Ghana
B .Mali
C. Kanem-Barnu
D. The Mossi States
E. Songhai
III. African Slave Trade and Territorial Dismemberment of Africa
A. Middle Passage
B. Effects of Slave Trade on Africa and the West
IV. Slavery in the Western Hemisphere
A. Indentured Servitude vs. Chattel Slavery
B. Problems and Accomplishments of Slaves in the West
C. Black Resistance to Slavery
1. Gabriel Prosser Plot in Virginia in 1800
   2. Denmark Vesey's Resistance in 1822 in South Carolina
   3. Nat Turner's Rebellion in Virginia in 1831
   4. Black and White Abolitionists
   a. Sojourner Truth
   b. Harriet Tubman
   c. Frederick Douglass

d. Elijah Lovejoy

e. William Lloyd Garrison

V. Black Participation in the Revolutionary War, War of 1812, U.S. - Mexican War, Civil War and subsequent wars after the Civil War

VI. Reconstruction and Its Aftermath

VII. Rise of Black Colleges and Universities

VIII Black Migration to the North and Founding of Black Self- help organization

A.NAACP – 1909

B. Urban League – 1910

C.U universal Negro Improvement Association

D.SCLC

E.PUSH

IX. Prominent Black Advocates of Political, Educational, and Economic Power for Black Americans before World War I

A. Dr. William E. B. DuBois

B. Booker T. Washington

C. James Weldon Johnson

D. Dr. John Hope Franklin

E. William Monroe Trotter

F. Dr. Lillie Carroll Jackson

G. Dr. Mary McCleod Bethune

H. Dr. Mordecai W. Johnson

I. A. Phillip Randolph

J. Dr. Dorothy Height

K. Dr. Martin Luther King, Jr.

L. Whitney Young

M. Malcolm X

N. Adam Clayton Powell

0. Walter White

P. Dr. Benjamin Hooks

Q. Dr. John E. Jacob

R. Reverend Jesse L. Jackson

X. Black Participation in the Harlem Renaissance

A. Music

B. Poetry

C. Art

D. Sculpture

E. Education

XI. Black Participation in Contemporary Wars

A .World War II

B. Korean War

C. Vietnam War

XII. Contemporary Leaders in the struggle for Human and Civil Rights

XIII. Black Americans in the Computer Information Age

STRATEGIES AND TECHNIQUES FOR DEVELOPING AND IMPLEMENTING AN AFROCENTRIC PROGRAM

It must be borne in mind, given the historic neglect, indifference and exclusion of Afro centric education in the curricula of most of the 16,000 school districts which comprise our nation's network of public schools serving 41 million students, that it will take risk-taking, courage and persistence to bring Afrocentric education into the educational mainstream. I believe the following six steps, as a minimum, are imperative:

1. A COMPREHENSIVE ANALYSIS OF THE SCHOOL SYSTEM'S CURRICULA TO DETERMINE IF THE CONTRIBUTIONS OF BLACK AMERICANS ARE DEPICTED IN A FACTUAL MANNER IN-DEPTH AND REALISTICALLY.

2. INSIST THAT SCHOOLADMINISTRATORS, WHERE DEFICITS EXIST, DEVELOP AN AFROCENTRIC PROGRAM.

3. REQUEST THE LOCAL BOARD OF EDUCATION, AS A MATTER OF POLICY, TO MANDATE, AS A REQUIREMENT FOR ALL STUDENTS AN AFROCENTRIC PROGRAM. BEYOND MULT-ETHNIC/ MULTICULTURAL PROGRAMS, AN IN-DEPTH, FACTUAL AND REQUIRED SYSTEMIC AND INCLUSIVE PROGRAM SHOULD BE SET IN PLACE FOR ALL STUDENTS. BLACK STUDENTS NEED SUCH PROGRAMS TO ENHANCE BOTH KNOWLEDGE AND SELF-ESTEEM; WHITE STUDENTS, IN ORDER TO OBTAIN FIRST-HAND KNOWLEDGE OF THE PROBLEMS, PAST AND PRESENT WHICH WEIGH HEAVILY AND DISPROPORTIONATELY ON BLACK AMERI¬CANS.

4. INSIST THAT TEXTBOOKS AND AUDIOVISUAL MATERIALS ARE PURCHASED WHICH PORTRAY THE RACIAL AND CULTURAL DI¬VERSITY OF OUR NATION.

5. INSIST ON STAFF DEVELOPMENT FOR ALL TEACHERS ON THE HISTORY AND CULTURE OF BLACK AMERICANS.

6. INSIST THAT CAREFUL MONITORING AND EVALUATION OF AFROCENTRIC PROGRAMS TAKE PLACE IN ORDER TO DETERMINE IF APPROPRIATE INSTRUCTION; IN FACT, IS GOING FORWARD IN THE CLASSROOM.

The extent to which Afrocentric programs go forward in an efficacious manner will be determined, in reality, by the extent to which Black parents in majority Black school districts are willing to make a commitment for socio-racial inclusion. Failure to act decisively and systematically will condemn another generation of Black youngsters to pain, low self-concept, disillusionment, and failure.

For the sake of clarity, educators need to agree on a workable definition of the terms in this debate. When we talk about an Afrocentric curriculum, what, in reality, do we mean? I believe what is required is a definition of the African experience that provides a factual account of Black Americans' accomplish-in cuts, travel and culture in a coherent manner and that also illuminates Blacks' interactions with other people on Earth.

At bottom, the goal of an Afrocentric curriculum should be not so much to supplant the present "Euro-centric" teaching of history, but rather to portray both U.S. and world history more inclusively and fairly.

I feel a sense of *déjà vu* over much of the current discussion. In 1969 I was link asked to develop a plan for what was then termed a "multi-ethnic/ multicultural, curriculum" for the Baltimore City Public Schools. That assignment led to the implementation in 1972 of one of the first social studies curriculums in the country to provide a factual, comprehensive portrayal of the contributions of Black Americans and other ethnic groups to U.S. and world history.

There's been a failure of some teachers in some schools to teach the pre-program of studies in a sustained and orderly manner.

I have little doubt that if students were being taught the present curriculum in a consistent, thorough manner, the picture of Black Americans that emerged would portray them positively and fully. But all programs must be monitored closely to ensure that the prescribed curriculum is in fact being taught, and in some cases it isn't.

As large urban school systems across the country become predominantly black, there is a tendency to call for "Afrocentric curriculums." This is essentially a political demand. Citizen groups now are calling for greater depth and breadth in teaching of the African and Afro-American experience to reflect the changing racial composition of the schools.

Accompanying the demand for political empowerment is a new emphasis on intellectual empowerment, which expresses itself in the call for using an Afrocentric curriculum to foster a deeper understanding of Black Americans" culture and the African roots of Black Americans before the era of the slave trade which began in the 15th century.

Finally, Afrocentric instruction is viewed as a means of instilling group pride and self-esteem among young Black Americans in order to encourage them to master the intellectual skills and habits of mind they will need to compete successfully in today's competitive job market.

We must understand, however, that even as efforts are made to strengthen and expand the so-called Afrocentric curriculum, the histories of Black and White Americans are inextricably intertwined. Both must be taught inclusively and comprehensively if students are to receive a factual and useful appreciation of the past.

It takes enormous courage and intellectual fortitude to teach the history of this country as it really is, as opposed to some sanitized, idealized version of the past. For far too long, unfortunately, we have been satisfied to teach dogmas from whence cometh no truth.

The Baltimore Evening Sun May 15, 1991

37 Years after the Brown Decision: Still Separate, Still Unequal

Friday's 37th anniversary of the Supreme Court's historic *Brown* decision, which declared racial segregation unconstitutional in the public schools, will be observed with very scant attention, hoopla or ceremonial proclamations and speeches.

As it does in 1991, the *Brown* decision in 1954 caused national ambivalence and apprehension. In fact, the decision reflected a kind of unsettling duality insofar as Black and White citizens were concerned. Blacks greeted the ruling by and large, with jubilation and euphoria; Whites, especially in the South, greeted it with brooding unease and incredulity. The violence, obfuscation massive resistance and ignominious "freedom of choice," plans to minimize" school desegregation would come after the Supreme Court ruled that desegregation must proceed with "all deliberate speed."

Baltimore actually had begun desegregation in 1963, two years before Brown, when 16 carefully chosen Blacks were admitted to Poly in a move orchestrated by the city branch of the NAACP, led by Juanita Jackson Mitchell and Thurgood Marshall. (Marshall addressed the school board just before it voted.) The rationale was that there was no pre-engineering curriculum available in what was called the "Division of Colored Schools." The same school board however, denied black admission to Western High School on the grounds that a program for academically able Black girls was available at Douglass High School.

Two years later and almost immediately after the *Brown* decision-a committee to study desegregation was appointed only three days after the ruling and the final vote was taken June 3-Baltimore became the nation's first legally segregated school system to comply with the high court's edict. With the exception of a vociferous group of parents and students at Southern High School, desegregation preceded very smoothly, thanks in part to the evenhanded management of Superintendent John Fischer.

But while it is true that official segregation ended in Baltimore and across the nation, separate and unequal education prevails 37 hears later for Black, Hispanic and Native American children. Why? Because there is a national disinclination to support equity and excellence to all schools and because Whites and Blacks alike are fleeing the urban centers, leaving them without the funds needed to operate quality schools.

The *Brown* decision was both a blessing and a bane. It was a blessing because the official separation of schoolchildren came to a merciful end. But in the long run, many Blacks paid a price. Thirty-seven years later we see the "brain drain" of black students and teachers to predominantly white schools. We see the virtual elimination of Black principals, except in urban schools.

Still, I believe the *Brown* decision of 1954 was just and proper in spite of the setbacks and difficulties of the present. It offered hope to Blacks and other minorities across the nation. There remains, amid the bleakness, a basis for hope that equality and excellence in public education will become realities for all children

Inspiring Airlift

Editor:

Israel's airlift of over 14,000 Ethiopian Jews for repatriation in Israel, in view of the deadly civil war in Ethiopia, was highly magnanimous, timely and inspirational.

I rejoice in the Israeli government's decision to move expeditiously, massively and efficaciously to render assistance to the beleaguered Ethiopian Jews.

I, too, hope that the temporary truce arranged in London between the warring parties in Ethiopia will bring surcease and peace to the Ethiopians who remain in their indigenous land.

Peace, freedom and prosperity are long overdue throughout Ethiopia.
Israel's bold and humanitarian gesture fully supports the sage counsel of the prophet Micah in daring "to do justly, to love mercy, and to walk humbly with thy God."

Kudos to Israel.

Presented to the Sojourner-Douglass College Annual
Academic Convocation - June 27, 1991

The Congruence of Academic Excellence with Cultural Imperatives

The Sojourner-Douglass College is most deserving of commendation in its creative, intrepid and sedulous pursuit of truth and willingness to involve the broader Baltimore community in serious and substantive discussion of urgent and vital contemporary issues. The selection of the topic, "The Congruence of Academic Excellence with Cultural Imperatives," is highly fitting and proper.

Very briefly because of the constraints of time and the desire for dialogical interaction with my fellow-panelists and the audience, I have developed my presentation from the perspective of the critical responsibility to utilize knowledge to serve societal needs. My remarks will center, essentially, on Black Americans in view of the lugubrious, worsening and saturnine socio-economic, political and educational status of over 30 million Black Americans. **The statistics on the Black America, restated at the meeting of the 21st Century Commission on the African American Male on May 22-24, 1991 in Washington, D.C. are highly troubling and ominous for both Black Americans and our nation; 25 percent of young Black males between 23 and 29 are in prison (609,000), more Black males are incarcerated or at some point in the criminal justice system than enrolled in institutions of higher education; Black men aged 15 to 24 are six times more likely to be killed than other Americans of similar age; 40 percent of Black males are functionally illiterate; unemployment rates for Black adult males is 12.2 percent as contrasted with 5.5 percent for White Americans and for Black teenagers the unemployment rates approach 40 percent compared with 15 percent of all White teenagers; 42.7 of all Black children under 18 are in poverty; the life expectancy for Black citizens is 65.2 compared to 72.2 for White citizens.** In short, in the most prosperous and powerful nation in the world, 12 percent of its population, or over 30 million Black citizens are on the edge of the socio-economic and educational precipice.

As academics or persons wedded to the world of ideas, we have a moral ethical obligation not only to seek truth and illumine it, but to use the fruits of our scholarly labors in an active, pragmatic and palpable way to elevate and sustain the human condition. I believe, given the immense needs of Black, Hispanic and poor persons in our nation and throughout the world, an unconditional categorical imperative is needed, as described by Immanuel Kant, to effect an action-based linkage between knowledge and service. We, too, I believe, have an obligation to respond actively, innovatively and constructively to what Dr. Martin Luther King, Jr. often referred to as the "fierce urgency of now."

I offer three perspectives necessary for societal progress, renewal and unification.

The epistemological dimension centers on the knowledge domain and its uses. Knowledge must be applied in understanding the richness and diversity of Black life and history within a world perspective, or Weltanschauung, to understand and appreciate the present and to develop creative hunches and applications for the future. *The ingestion of banks of knowledge without functional or practical applications is a sure prescription for frustration, pain and failure.*

The ontological emphasis concerns socio-economic, political, cultural and educational realities. What, in fact, as we approach the pulsating and tantalizing challenges and opportunities of the 21st Century, is the reality of being Black, Hispanic, Native American or poor in a predominantly White American? To what extent, in recent times, after the passage of the 1957, 1960, and 1964 Civil Rights Acts, the 1965 Voting Rights Act and the 1968 Fair Housing Act, has the American stated ethos of "Liberty and Justice for All" or "Equal Justice Under Law" become a reality for non-white Americans? Why does President George Walker Bush, even after bipartisan support in Congress, continue to speak, mendaciously and unfairly, of the proposed Civil Rights Act of 1991 as a quota bill? Knowledge, truth and action must be brought to bear synergistically in support of wholeness in the body politic and to foster and maintain equality of opportunity and social justice for all.

The axiological pertains to values. What values do we proclaim and practice as a nation? The values of truth, justice, fairness, equal chance, and respect for differences need careful reexamination in terms of the fact versus truth and the ideal versus reality.

The "best and brightest" in our nation, transcending the synthetic factors of color, race, gender and ethnicity, must be used in a maximal and open relationship to empower, transform and liberate the talents and abilities resident in all persons. The liberation or emancipation of the mind and human possibilities, here on earth, and getting people think and act for themselves, are overriding priorities or imperatives.

Dr. Carter G. Woodson, universally regarded as the "Father of Black History" and the founder of the national Association for the Study of Afro-American Life and History in 1915, provides an apt and sage conclusion for my presentation:

> *When you control a man's thinking you do not have to worry about his actions. You do not have to tell him to stand here or go yonder. He will find his "proper place" and will stay in it. You do not need to send him to the back door. In fact, if there is no back door, he will cut one for his special benefit. His education makes it necessary. (1)*

Let us be about the supreme task to help all persons to think for themselves and to become, in a free and equal society, autonomous beings. It is a mission worthy of all who believe that "The truth shall set you free."

The Afro-American - Baltimore- July 20, 1991

Thomas Nomination Should Go Forward

The nomination of Judge Clarence Thomas by President George Herbert Walker Bush to succeed the venerable, redoubtable and highly respected Justice Thurgood Marshall as a member of the United States Supreme Court has been an occasion for consternation and cataclysmic public reaction throughout the United States.

On balance, however, most Black Americans, according to informal polls and public comments, although not jubilant, support and believe that Judge Thomas will be confirmed by the Senate Judiciary Committee, which is chaired by Senator Joseph Biden of Delaware.

I am neither enchanted nor enamored of Judge Thomas' ideological perspectives, to date, on affirmative action, equality of opportunity and First Amendment rights, including a woman's right to choice, but I believe his nomination, making him the second Black American to occupy a seat on the Supreme Court in its 202-year existence, should go forward.

I do not believe, however, as put forth by President Bush, that Judge Thomas, based upon judicial experience, sensitivity to the needs of the elderly, minorities and women, and academic-intellectual perspicacity, was the "best" person to succeed Justice Marshall. The cardinal and pragmatic reality is that Judge Thomas was the choice of President Bush because of his conservatism and kinship with Bush's philosophical ideology on socio-racial issues.

I believe that Judge Thomas will be confirmed because the numbers are in place in the Senate, and I believe in the capacity of people to undergo sociopolitical redemption and to grow. I recall when Thurgood Marshall, then Chief Counsel for the NAACP, argued the momentous *Brown vs. Board of Education of Topeka* decision in 1952-53; there were three justices on the nine-member Supreme Court from the South who were on the Supreme Court.

The justices from the South were Justices Tom C. Clark from Texas; Stanley F. Reed from Kentucky; and Hugo L. Black from Alabama. These three justices joined with their six other brethren of the U.S. Supreme Court to render, unanimously, the renowned and epochal *Brown* decisions of 1954 and 1955 which paved the way for Clarence Thomas and countless other Black and non-White children and youths to enjoy the opportunity of desegregated education in our nation's public schools.

Just as Justices Black, Clark and Reed expanded their thinking as members of the court, as was true of other Supreme Court justices, I believe that Judge Thomas, interpreting an elastic document, our national Constitution, will not be stultified or ossified with respect to his socio-economic and constitutional beliefs, but, too, will grow and remember his peculiar historical roots.

The Baltimore Evening Sun - August   28, 1991

Blacks and Jews

Editor: I am pained and appalled by the tragic deaths in Brooklyn and the subsequent obstreperous and violent clashes between groups of Blacks and Jews. It is most heartening that Mayor David Dinkins has moved with alacrity, directness and power to end the confrontations between Blacks and Hasidic Jews and urged Black and Jewish leaders and lay persons to restore calm, respect and community pride and unity.

It, too, is equally disquieting and a source of dismay, given the historic and long-standing bonds of amity and unity which have historically existed in this nation between Blacks and Jews in our common struggle for social justice, human dignity and equality of opportunity for all, to observe the present fractious and divisive conflict in Brooklyn.

I am confident that common sense and rationality will prevail in Brooklyn and the tensions and hostilities of long standing will abate and pass over. It is, I believe, an ethical-moral imperative that Blacks and Jews work together, not only in Brooklyn, but throughout our nation for a more caring, just and equal body politic.

Afro American - Baltimore - September 7, 1991

Judge Clarence Thomas Revisited

President George Herbert Walker Bush's nomination of Judge Clarence Thomas to succeed Associate Justice Thurgood Marshall as a member of the U.S. Supreme Court has been the occasion for much pain, ambivalence and travail among 32 million Black Americans.

This lamentable state of affairs exists, to a Law degree, because Judge Thomas' public pronouncements and writings relative to affirmative action and equality of opportunity have not been supportive of demonstrable socio-economic justice and equality of opportunity for all Americans.

In this sense, the NAACP, as a matter of fundamental principle, rationality and decency, took appropriate action in opposing Judge Thomas's confirmation as an associate justice of the Supreme Court, as a matter of fundamental principle, after considerable deliberation and a direct meeting with Judge Thomas.

I believe, too, as I have indicated in a previous column, that Judge Thomas will be confirmed unless the proverbial "smoking gun" or more damaging evidence is uncovered in the confirmation proceedings which will soon be underway.

The Senate Judiciary Committee, headed by Senator Joseph Biden of Delaware, will have full and open hearings on Judge Thomas' nomination and send its recommendation to the full Senate to work its legislative will.

Organizations and persons who desire to make their positions known, pro or con, germane to Judge Thomas' fitness for the Supreme Court should communicate with Senator Biden's Judiciary Committee.

I, too, wish to reaffirm that I am not enchanted with nor enamored with Judge Thomas' public pronouncements against affirmative action, his reactionary and dilatory actions for human and civil rights while serving as the head of the Equal Employment Opportunity Commission, and his amorphous and arcane references to "natural law."

Moreover, I do not believe, as President Bush has indicated, that he was the "best" person to succeed associate justice Marshall.

There are a number of seminal, prescient and superior Black legal scholars and jurists such as Derrick Bell of the Harvard Law School and Federal Judge A. Leon Higgenbotham who are highly respected and admired.

The chief problem, however, is that progressive, highly able and forward-looking persons like Dr. Bell and Judge Higginbotham do not comport with the conservative ideology of President Bush.

As we oppose the confirmation of Judge Thomas as a matter of egalitarian principles and simple justice, in keeping with the ethical-moral tenets which have served as a bedrock for witness and action by the NAACP for a just and equal society since its founding in 1909, we must deplore and forswear individuals and groups which refer to Judge Thomas in highly personal, invidious and pejorative terms (viz., "snake," modern day Judas," "quisling," etc.).

Judge Thomas should either be supported or opposed in terms of his ability, temperament, and fitness for the Supreme Court.

As efforts are mounted to testify against Judge Thomas, as a matter of principle and fairness, we must not lose sight of other urgent and pressing issues which confront Black Americans as reflected in worsening employment and underemployment levels, shoddy and unequal education, inadequate housing and soaring health costs and insufficient or non-existent health coverage.

In this conjunction, it is tragic indeed that as we have just completed the celebration of Labor Day, a disproportionate number of Black Americans are experiencing a Depression and not a recession.

We must not allow the nomination of Judge Thomas to divide us and lessen our efforts for other urgent matters.

Presented At the Annual Meeting of the Black Ecumenical
Advocacy Ministry (BEAM), Howard University, Washington,
D.C. - September 9, 1991

The Black Family in the United States During A Period of Crisis and Travail: Strategies for Survival and Progress

Introduction

The Black family, to be sure, as a result of negative and invidious centripetal and centrifugal forces, is under siege. The reality, spanning denominational lines and involving ecclesiastical officials, educators and highly committed and respected lay person, is palpable evidence that you believe in the possibilities for renewal, rejuvenation and progress for the Black family. You, too, I believe, provide a contemporary dimension to the historic proposition that "Troubles are not new to us as a people." We must dare, in season and out of season, to push forward and upward for our collective spiritual and material salvation and progress on the "Spaceship Earth."

It is enormously fitting and proper that you as church folk have taken the leadership, as has been indicative of the past, in providing reliable, audacious, believable and achievable initiatives in support of the recrudescence and uplift of over 33 million Black people in our nation. *The Black church has served, past and present, as a steadying, reassuring, catalytic and redoubtable energizer, comforter and anchor for Black people during their ignominious and bestial transport from "Mother Africa" to the western hemisphere. In slavery and in freedom, the Black church has provided for Black families, in varying forms, spiritual and psychological succor and relief necessary for physical support and survival during trying, cumbersome and vexatious times.* The Black church, the one autonomous, independent and potent institution within the Black social order, represents a vitalizing beacon of hope and opportunity for Black people. As we meet here in the salubrious and comforting academic-intellectual environs of Howard University, so rich in our history, we must ever be mindful of from whence we have come and where, if we are to keep the Black family vibrant and progressive, we must go in order to achieve full socio-economic parity in the American body politic. The socio-economic, political and educational stakes are high, and we must view the present societal challenges and problems as opportunities for serious strategizing and action.

The late Dr. Martin Luther King, Jr., a towering stalwart in the universal struggle for human and civil rights during a period of painful and reflective thought during the turbulent 1960's, observed: "Every man [woman] should have something he'd die for. A man who won't die for something is not fit to live." It is, however, not the focus of this paper to urge those of you assembled here in this august and majestic setting to make the ultimate terrestrial sacrifice. The primary focus of this paper is three-fold: (1) to provide a brief historical overview of Black people achieving against the odds in slavery and beyond; (2) to provide a brief description of critical problems which impinge on Black people today; (3) to recommend specific and concrete strategies for socio-economic, political and educational regeneration, renewal and renaissance

FROM WHENCE WE HAVE COME

As we consider the Black family, we must ever be mindful of our historical roots. Black family life and socio-economic, political and educational institutions flourished in "Mother Africa" long before the development of Europe. In 1441, with the arrival of the Portuguese, life in Africa was never to be the same. According to Elizabeth G. Donnan, *Documents Illustrative of the African Slave Trade* and William Edward Burghardt DuBois, *Suppression of the African Slave Trade,* over 50 million to 100 million Africans were expatriated or removed from their homeland. Approximately 15 million Africans died in the heinous Triangular Trade. In an effort to destroy Black family life and cohesion, Black persons were deliberately, systematically and cruelly separated by the slave dealers in terms of their tribal and linguistic background. The fundamental purpose was to prevent communication and a sense of unity among the Africans. The overarching purpose, of course, was to break their spirit and force them to accept a dehumanized status and perform as docile and passive "hewers of wood and drawers of water." In spite of the monstrous treatment that our forebears endured, they refused to accept themselves as inanimate objects or to allow, as a collective group, their spirit to be broken. *Then, too, we should always remember that the greatness of our nation is due in very large measure to the ineradicable and monumental contributions of Black people, in slavery and freedom, in the face of awesome odds.*

The assault on Black people continued in the New World. Our nation, historically, has been resistant to change and to new arrivals that did not fit the mold of White Anglo-Saxon Protestants (i.e., WASPS). A comment of Oscar Handlin is probing and revealing germane to some early White immi¬grants:

> *Learned men had told me they were hardly human at all; their head shapes were different, their bodily structure faulty, the weight of their brains deficient. If they were Italians, they were not really like the Italians, they were not really like the Italians who had a claim to the mantle of Rome; if they were Greeks, and they were not genuine Greeks, descended from the Hellenes. (1)*

Black arrivals to the New World received the greatest vilification and traducement. Thomas Jefferson, the third President of our nation and the "Sage of Monticello" would declare:

> *Comparing them (i.e., slaves) by their faculties of memory, reason and imagination, it appears to me, that in memory they are equal to Whites; in reason much inferior, as I think one could scarcely be found capable of tracing and comprehending the investigations of Euclid-in imagination they are dull, tasteless and anomalous. (2)*

John Hope Franklin, one of our nation's premier historians, records, at a much later period and in less elegant language, a comment of a White racist by the name of Edwin Clifford Holland:

> *Let it never be forgotten, that "our Negroes" are freely the JACOBINS of the country; that they are the ANARCHISTS OF CIVILIZED SOCIETY, and the BARBARIANS WHO WOULD, IF THEY COULD, BECOME THE DESTROYERS OF OUR RACE. (3)*

Tirades against Black people reached a new high before the turn of the twentieth century. Congressman John Sharpe Williams, in a caustic address on December 20, 1898, asserted:

> *You could shipwreck 10,000illiterate White Americans on a desert island, and in three weeks they would have a fairly good*

government, conceived and administered upon fairly democratic lines. You could shipwreck 10,000 Negroes (sic), every one of whom was a graduate of Harvard University, and in less than three years, they would have retrograded governmentally, half of the men would have been killed, and the other half would have two wives apiece. (4)

In terms of the political sphere, Senator Ben Tillman of South Carolina would continue the attack:

We have done our best (i.e., disenfranchisement) of Black voters in South Carolina. We have scratched our heads to find out how we could eliminate the last one of them (i.e., Black voters). We stuffed ballot boxes; we shot them (i.e., Black citizens). We are not ashamed of it. (5)

In spite of the vicissitudes, obfuscation, denial of fundamental freedom and human dignity, and violence, our people have continued the tiptoeing and inexorable march toward full freedom, social justice and equality of opportunity in our native land. *We should exult and take hope, for although tattered and battered, the Black family, through it all, remains firmly intact.*

PRESENT DAY CHALLENGES

The factor of institutional and operational racism, exclusion from the socio-economic, educational and political mainstream, and a worsening economy serve to bedevil and exacerbate the manifold problems which weigh heavily on 32 million Black people. We have reached a lamentable and painful historical juncture where the majority White population is either disinclined or apathetic relative to the continuing socio-economic, political and educational subordinating of Black people is concerned. After the passage, after the immense struggle, pain and sacrifice of the 1957, 1960, 1964 civil rights bills and the 1965 Voting Rights Act and the 1968 Fair Housing Act, amended in 1989, the majority White population has not been supportive of additional civil rights legislation. President George Herbert Walker Bush, playing to the fears of White people through the mythological and vacuous references to "quotas," has been successful in defeating the 1990 Civil Rights Act and, at this point in time, is working either to defeat the Civil Rights Act of 1991 or to eviscerate it.

The inability of Black Americans, at a time of unprecedented national prosperity, to have socio-economic, educational and political parity, has been devastating for Black family life and community solidarity and unity. Even as we meet here, the statistics on Black America are grim, disquieting and ominous: *25 percent of young Black males between 23 and 29 are in prison (i.e., 609,000); more Black males are incarcerated at some point in the crimi¬nal justice system than enrolled in institutions of higher education; Black men aged 15 to 24 are six times more likely to be killed than other Americans of similar age; 40 percent of Black males are functionally illiterate; the unemployment rate for Black adult males is 12.2percent contrasted with 5.5percent for White Americans, and for Black teenagers the unemployment rate approaches 40 percent compared with 15 percent of all white teenagers; 42.7 of all Black children under 18 are in poverty; the life expectancy for black citizens is 65.2 per cent compared to 72.2 percent for White citizens. In short, in the most prosperous and powerful nation in the world, 12 percent of its population, or over 32 million Black citizens are on the edge of a socio-economic and educational precipice. This, to be sure, is a national disgrace.*

WHAT WE MUST DO: ACTION-ORIENTED RECOMMENDATIONS

As we deliberate in the manifold and compelling sessions here at Howard University, we must not allow ourselves to become enchanted with our grandiloquent and soaring rhetoric nor allow ourselves to become immobilized through what Martin Luther King, Jr. described as the "paralysis of analysis." Moreover, even as we understand the formidable factors of institutional racism and exclusion which have restricted and constricted our participation in the American body politic, we must still dare to think anew and match our rhetoric with demonstrable deeds and witness for relief and progress.

I, too, hope, in your group and plenary sessions, that you will not permit yourselves to become bogged down discussing the merits or demerits of Judge Clarence Thomas' fate before the Senate Judiciary Committee headed by Senator Joe Biden of Delaware. Judge Thomas' heroic and glowing rise from abject poverty in Pinpoint, Georgia, through hard work, self-reliance and perseverance, is a source of pride and admiration. However, his experience mirrors that of a vast number of nameless Black citizens, some of you present today, who have achieved a measure of success against stupendous societal odds. To the extent that Judge Thomas has not been supportive of equal employment opportunity and women's rights and possesses an amorphous and nebulous view of natural rights, as revealed in his writing and public utterances, he should not, as a matter of fundamental principle, go forward. Whatever the outcome on Judge Thomas, we must mobilize our best thinking and resources in support of the Civil Rights Act of 1991, jobs, national health insurance, high quality education, humane and progressive care for the elderly, and decent, safe and sanitary housing for all.

CONCLUSION

The problems which plague the Black family must not be viewed in isolation but holistically or comprehensively. Education and jobs represent the *sine qua non* or centerpieces in the resuscitation, renewal and progress of the Black family. Mindful of this, I wrote in 1985:

> *Black churches, parents, civic and fraternal groups and professional groups must be involved deeply and pervasively in helping to deliver equality of opportunity and educational excellence to their children and youths and for themselves. Self-help, educational programs and tutorial and enrichment activities stressing racial pride and academic and vocational skill development should be a vital, required and ongoing part of all Black organizations. (6)*

Finally, in support of the vitality, vibrancy and progress of the Black family, we must dare to be risk-takers and to think for ourselves. Carter Godwin Woodson, widely regarded as the "Father of Black History," states the case cogently and aptly:

> *The problem of holding the Negro down, therefore, is easily solved. When you control a man's thinking you do not have to worry about his actions. You do not have to tell him to stand here or go yonder. He will find his "proper place" and will stay in it. You do not need to send him to the back door. In fact, if there is no door, he will cut one for his special benefit. His education makes it necessary. (7)*

The time is not at hand for all of us to answer the "Macedonian Call" in contemporary times in behalf of a people who have been "buked and scorned" in the historic and universal quest for social justice, equality of opportunity and socio-economic, educational and political parity. *I urge you now, pregnant with challenge and opportunity, to dare not to become a part of the litany of those who whine or echo the proposition of the endangered Black male or Black people.*

We must repudiate and forswear this mythology, necrology and affirm hope, determination and high quality survival and progress in succeeding against the odds and making 'bricks without straw" compatible with our glorious history.

The Afro American – Baltimore - November 2, 1991

The Civil Rights Act of 1991

After a long and unnecessary delay, the Civil Rights Act of 1991 is about to be passed, with modifications, by the Congress and sent to President George Herbert Walker Bush for his signature.

The legislation, in reality, parallels the Civil Rights Act of 1990 which was vetoed by President Bush with his misleading, inaccurate and mendacious references to a "quota bill." The Civil Rights Act of 1990 was not a "quota bill," nor is the Civil Rights Act of 1991, as is well known by President Bush.

It is demonstrably clear, given the pernicious and subtle expansion of institutional racism and sexism in our nation, that Black and non-White Americans and women, in particular, needed relief and assurance that our nation would not countenance a retreat on elemental human and civil rights.

The passage of the Civil Rights Act of 1991 will signal anew that equality of opportunity will not be denied persons in the workplace because of race or gender.

In view of President Bush's initial recalcitrance to the Civil Rights Act of 1991, Republican Senator John C. Danforth of Missouri and Democratic Senator Edward Kennedy of Massachusetts are deserving of commendation and praise for their singular, persistent and indefatigable leadership, in concert with members of their respective political parties, in sheep-herding the bill through the Senate.

Black and non-White Americans and women have every reason to exult and rejoice when the Civil Rights Act of 1991 is signed belatedly into law by President Bush.

The essential elements of the Civil Rights Act of 1991, in view of recent reactionary decisions of the Supreme Court pertaining to racism in the workplace, will make it easier for Black and non-White citizens to prevail or win discrimination suits and enable victims of sex discrimination in the workplace to sue for damages. Financial awards to women who successfully prove sex discrimination will be limited by law.

The Civil Rights Act of 1991 could not come at a better time for Black Americans who have been, to a very substantial degree, in a state of economic depression for the past 20 years.

While White America is currently experiencing a recession, and even President Bush now accepts this reality, Black America is in the worst economic doldrums since the great depression of the 1930's. Additionally, over one-third of the 32 million Black Americans in our nation are in a state of poverty and 42,7 percent of all Black children throughout our nation live in a state of poverty This bleak and lugubrious situation, coupled with other societal pathologies (viz., Black-on-Black violence, escalating substance abuse, functional illiteracy, widening unemployment-underemployment, etc.), will worsen before it improves.

The Civil Rights Act of 1991, to be sure, will not be a panacea or an instant cure for the multiplicity of problems, internal and external, which devolve on 32 million Black citizens, but it does offer a palpable and concrete sign of HOPE.

In this conjunction, I was pleased to hear John E. Jacob, president of the National Urban League, renew his call for a "National Domestic Marshall Plan." We possess the human and monetary resources, as the most prosperous nation in the world, to transform HOPE into ABLE and TANGIBLE SOCIO-ECONOMIC PROGRAMS. WHAT IS REQUIRED IS A NATIONAL MOBILIZATION OF WILL AND RESOURCES.

As I think of the possibilities inherent in the 1991 Civil Rights Act, I am reminded of former Representative Parren J. Mitchell's and Sister Katherine Corr's masterful, seminal and marvelous conceptualization and execution of the Baltimore-led "March on Washington to Save Our Cities" on Saturday, October 12, 1991.

The Civil Rights Act of 1991 points us, at a critical juncture, in the right direction: LET US DARE TO SEIZE THE MOMENT AND PUSH FORWARD AND UPWARD.

1992

Presented at a City wide Meeting of the Baltimore Branch,
Association for the Study of Afro-American Life and History -
January 14, 1992

Racial Equality in America:
A Far Distant Shore

Two clear, palpable and ineluctable elements of the human condition are the issues of CHANGE and RESPONSE. The rapidity and dizzying tempo of change often times makes it immensely difficult for a man/woman both here in the United States and throughout the world community to make rational, secure and effective adjustments. Throughout human history diversified people have striven to achieve a balance and equanimity with natural forces and to grapple with and set forth tentative answers to three fundamental and universal questions: WHO AM I? WHERE AM I GOING? HOW DO I GET THERE? It is not the intent of this paper to attempt answers to these three ancient and historic questions, but to provide, within an AFRO-CENTRIC or Black perspective, an assessment of our standing as Black people within the American body politic and the necessity for caring and outreach in a broader sphere.

Dr. Howard Thurman, a renowned theologian, preacher, scholar and educator, provides a steadying, inspirational and absorbing challenge in speaking of the need for security and firm support in a challenging society:

> It is a strange freedom to be adrift in the world of men without a sense of anchor anywhere. Always there is the need of mooring, the need for the firm grip on something that is rooted and will not give. The urge to be accountable to some, to know that beyond the individual there is an answer that must be given-this cannot be denied. (1)

Dr. Thurman concludes on this point:

> The very spirit of a man tends to panic from the desolation of going nameless up and down the streets of other minds where no

salutation greets and no friendly recognition makes secure. It is
a strange freedom to be adrift in the world of men. (2)

The paramount purpose of this paper is to provide an overview and analysis of the longstanding, virulent and deleterious effects of institutional and operational racism on Black Americans, past and present, and to show how Blacks have responded to the historic "troubles of the world" and a rapidly changing world order. Too often we have had simply the benefit of EUROCENTRIC (i.e., Caucasian) analyses with Blacks and non-whites portrayed as "invisible" or hopeless and "inferior" burdens of the world. My paper addresses the AFRO-CENTRIC focus in terms of three dimensions:

1. ONTOLOGICAL
2. AXILOGICAL
3. EPISTEMOLOGICAL
THE ONTOLOGICAL (REALITY) PERSPECTIVE

An understanding of the evolution, vicissitudes and progress of Black Americans, starting with "Mother Africa," is necessary in terms of appreciating the human condition of 32 million in our nation today. So many historians, either through ignorance or feelings of superiority, refuse to accept the luminous and extraordinary contributions of Black people in "Mother Africa" to world civilization. A major reason for this situation is that both institutional and operational racism was in vogue and practice when the Portuguese started the infamous and heinous system of human trafficking with the socio-economic penetration of Africa in 1442.

Winthrop D. Jordan provides a direct, pithy and pungent observation as to how Englishmen viewed Africans in his well-publicized book, White Over Black:

> *Far from isolating African heathenism as a separate characteristic, English travelers sometimes linked explicitly with barbarity and blackness. They already had classified Whites, in a mediating term among these impinging concepts-the devils. (3)*

White Over Black made the blatant comment of one observer:

> *"Negroes in, color so in condition are little other than a Devil incarnate. (4)*

An ethos had developed in Europe, long before the colonization of the Western Hemisphere, that Black people were a subhuman people and a burden on the world. White expresses the view cogently and directly:

> *The condition, of savagery—t he failure to be civilized— set Negroes apart from Englishmen in an ill-defined but crucial fashion. Africans were different, languages, government, morals. (5)*

The historical reality is that long before Europeans were considered "civilized" and arrived in Africa, the highly sophisticated and advanced African civilizations of Ghana, Mali, Songhai, Kenem-Bornu the Mossi States, among others, were firmly in place. The work of eminent and highly respected Black historians such as Drs. Carter G. Woodson, Charles H. Wesley, John Hope Franklin, Benjamin Quarles, Chancellor Williams and Ivan Sertima have documented the seminal and solid contributions of African civilizations before the arrivals of the Europeans in 1442. An understanding of this remarkable period of Black achievement in "Mother Africa" is essential to understanding the socio-economic, political, educational and cultural standing of 32 million Black Americans in our nation today.

A critical and vital factor that has prevented Black Americans from achieving parity, autonomy and power, past and present, has been an ancient racial bifurcation or duality; orchestrated, nurtured and sustained by the majority White society. Dr. William Edward Burghardt Dubois, scholar-historian extraordinaire, captured this American and world dilemma when he stated in Souls of Black Folk

> The history of the American Negro is the history of this strife— this longing to attain self-conscious manhood, to merge his double self into a better and truer self. In this merging he wishes neither of the older selves to be lost. He would not Africanize America, for America has too much to teach the world and Africa. He would not bleach his Negro soul in a flood of White Americanism, for he knows that Negro blood has a message for the world. He simply wishes to make it possible for a man to be both a Negro and an American, without being cursed upon by his fellows, without having the Doors of Opportunity closed roughly in his face. (6)

The crux of the matter, I believe, is stated by DuBois when he declares:

> *It is a peculiar sensation, this double-consciousness, this always looking at one's self through the eyes of others, of measuring one's soul by the tape of a world that looks on in amused contempt and pity. One ever feels his two-ness, an American, a Negro; two souls, two thoughts, two unreconciled strivings; two warring ideals in one dark body, whose dogged strength alone keeps it from being torn asunder. (7)*

The central and unsettling crisis of Black and non-White people in the United States and abroad, South Africa being an egregious example, is the condition of the racial duality or "two-ness" affirmed by DuBois over 88 years ago. Universal peace, brotherhood/sisterhood and amity will not go forward when over two-thirds of the world's five billion people are, by and large, in a position of institutional subordination and exclusion from the global main¬stream.

THE AXIOLOGICAL (VALUES) PERSPECTIVE

The values deemed as significant and worthy of emulation and, to a large degree, throughout the world, posit a fundamental proposition: If The Values Are Not European (i.e., White), Something Is Deficient or Wrong. In reality, it is the old practice of ethnocentrism in which the customs, traditions, mores and systems of belief are measured or gauged primarily in terms of White values, attitudes and systems of belief. The historical practices delineated earlier serve to reinforce, extend and buttress the mythological and specious view of White superiority. There are, in fact, no superior individuals within the general anthropological classification of humankind (viz., Mongoloid-Asian, Caucasoid, and Negroid). *There are, in fact, superior individuals within races, but there are no superior races.*

A major axiological dimension which courses through our history is the concept of the Protestant Ethic. Max Weber, a well-known German, popularized this ethos. The Protestant Ethic advances the proposition that through hard work-industry, frugality, education, adherence to church, dedication and persistence, among other gentle qualities, one can achieve success and fulfillment in the social order. The basic hamartia (i.e., fatal flaw) with Weberian principles is that it appertained, in the development of our nation, essen¬tially to WASPS (i.e., White Anglo-Saxon Protestants). While other White Southern and Eastern European Whites and people of other faiths (viz., Catholics, Jews, etc.), especially since 1945, have been brought within the rubric of the Protestant ethic in an operational sense, 32 million Black Americans, to a substantial degree, have been excluded.

Today, in the United States, over one-third, or 12 million, Black people live in poverty. When one considers the working poor among Black people, over 18 million Black citizens are either poor or a permanent underclass. In spite of the passage of epochal and forward-looking civil rights legislation (via, 1957,1960,1664,1965,1968), after enormously bitter and costly struggle and perseverance, the larger White society, as a group, still views 32 million Black people, as a group, as a suborder of human life and uneducable. This represents the tragic and lugubrious reality as we approach the promises, hopes and uncertainty of the 21st Century and untrammeled citizenship and equality of opportunity remains a far distant goal for Black Americans.

The remarkable Paul Robeson, in his masterful and evocative Here I Stand, provides a challenge to all who believe in the preciousness and indivisibility of freedom in speaking to a congressional committee in 1956:

> *I stand here struggling for the rights of my country. They are not in Mississippi. This is why I am here today. . . You want to shut up every colored person who wants to fight for the rights of his people. (8)*

Dr. Martin Luther King, Jr., Non-Violent Apostle of Change, in his world-acclaimed and powerful "Letter from Birmingham Jail," offers another view in support of universal human values and possibilities:

> *Let us all hope that the dark clouds of racial prejudice will soon pass away and the deep fog of misunderstanding will be lifted from our fear-drenched communities, and in some not too distant tomorrow the radiant stars of love and brotherhood will shine over our great nation with all their scintillating beauty. (9)*

The "scintillating beauty/ that King hoped for 28 years ago while in a Birmingham jail has not become a reality, neither in the United States nor in the world community. Man's inhumanity to man/woman continues, in various guises and manifestations, as the cardinal order of the day.

THE ESPITEMOLOGICAL (KNOWLEDGE) PERSPECTIVE

The old truism that "knowledge is power" certainly has validity and merit. However, I believe, it must be the right kind of knowledge within the educational process. Much of what passes for knowledge or learning in our nation's public schools and institutions of higher education is education subservience, docility and passivity. This condition is particularly acute for Black, Hispanic and Native Americans because of institutional subordination, exclusion and the racial "two-ness" in place before and after the settlement of the Western Hemisphere.

A formidable and urgent task for Black citizens in cooperation with progressive and fair-minded White citizens, and where and when possible, civic groups, politicians, sororities and fraternities, is to insist upon demonstrable educational excellence, equity and education that liberates the mind.

Dr. Carter Godwin Woodson, the venerable and world renowned "Father of Black History," provided a potent and sage observation in his seminal, *The Mis-Education of the Negro.* (10)

Woodson, of course, was illuminating education of subservience and control and not the emancipation of the mind and innate talents. He adds further evidence to this point in writing that education of control and docility crushes "the spark of genius in the Negro by making him feel that his race does not amount to much and never will measure up to the standards of other peoples." (11) Therefore, Blacks who are educated in this manner are "a hopeless liability of the race." (12)

Woodson's words, written 58 years ago, may appear harsh to some, but the elements of verisimilitude and historical accuracy, past and present, are undeniable and irrefutable. Since the epochal and momentous *Brown vs. Board of Education of Topeka*, decision of 1954, beginning with the shutdown of the Prince Edward County, Virginia Public Schools for five years, we have lost several generations of Black children through school shutdowns, shoddy and inferior education and widespread practices of suspension, expulsion and school dropouts/push outs nationally are Hispanic and Black students. The minimal knowledge and understandings acquired by these youngsters represent pass¬ports to failure and the socio-economic scrapheap.

The reality in the American social order, notwithstanding the grim warning of a "rising tide of mediocrity" contained in A Nation At Risk, published in 1983, is that little attention has been given to the enormous educational deficits and lack of equal opportunity for Black, Hispanic and poor children and youths. In point of fact, over 25 major reports have been written which, except in a few instances, give substantive and serious attention to lack of fiscal equity and opportunity for over 9 million Black children enrolled in our nation's public schools. This, to be sure, is a national disgrace and calamity.

In *Stony the Road: the Black American in the American Experience*, published in 1972, I addressed the need to confront educational inequality head on:

> We have an obligation to help make sense as we seek to transmit meaningful class exposures, traditions and knowledge of them (i.e., students). An index to our effectiveness will be evidenced in our efforts making sense to students as they grapple with heavy and unsettling social and economic problems not of their making. We must also make a sedulous effort to bring warmth and cheer to our classes—humanize them. Students may not, in fact, be able to comprehend the subject matter that we devoutly want them to know, but there should be no doubt that you cared—really cared—about each stu¬dent developing to his/her fullest extent. (13)

The problem of unequal educational opportunity for Black children and youths is further exacerbated by Depression levels of unemployment in urban centers, proliferating deaths and maiming occasioned by substance and alcohol abuse and a disproportionate number of fatalities from Acquired Immune Deficiency Syndrome (i.e., AIDS), escalating teenage pregnancies, and a gen¬eral alienation and bitterness toward the larger body politic.

In spite of the bleakness of the present situation, there is still a basis for hope though educational and economic empowerment. I am convinced that "Our nation's public schools can become beacons of hope, equality of opportunity and demonstrable excellence for all of our children and youths." (14) What is urgently needed is an audacious, systematic and persistent mobilization of will and human and monetary resources. (15)

DuBois, once again, offers a universal challenge:

> *I sit with Shakespeare and he winces not. Across the color line
> I move arm in arm with Balzac and Dumas, where smiling
> men and welcoming women glide in gilded halls. From out the
> caves of evening that swing between the strong-limbed earth and
> the tracery of the stars, I summon Aristotle and Aurelius and
> what soul I will, and they come all graciously with no scorn or
> condescension. So, wed with Truth, I dwell above the Veil. Is
> this the life you grudge us, O knightly America? .... Are you so
> afraid lest peering from this high Pisgah, between Philistine and
> Amalekite, we sight the Promised Land. (16)*

As must be evident in this paper, a Zeitgeist (i.e., Spirit of the times) hat is inhospitable and non-supportive of Black citizens is in place. However, troubles are not new to Black people. Black people, as in past times, oust summon the collective strength, ingenuity, spirit, will and resources, through it all, to press forward.

We must dare to take the leap of faith and maintain an unwavering faith in God as we move forward and upward in the American body politic and the world order.

While we have not achieved in our nation and the world, the "scintillating beauty that the Reverend Dr. King hoped for 28 years ago in Birmingham jail, we must, nonetheless, work unrelentingly and confidently for a mutual, just, humane and caring world order for the present and the future. It is a necessary task for all who believe in the primacy of human life, equal opportunity, fairness and global tranquility. Let us, at a late hour in human history, be on our way.

Presented to the Men's Council of Sargent Memorial Presbyterian Church on the Occasion of the 40th Annual Men's Council Communion Breakfast, Washington, D.C. -April 5, 1992

Dare To Care

I chose to speak on the topic, "Dare to Care," because an urgent need exists for us as Black men to become more actively involved in the life of our families and communities as strong and positive role models and mentors. As we face the multifaceted vicissitudes and problems which beset us as a people, it has become demonstrably clear that we must do more to help ourselves.

In this conjunction, I believe there are four critical elements that require our immediate attention. They are as follows:

I. KNOW YOUR ROOTS

When I speak of knowing one's roots, I am not talking about the practice of "fixing" someone through the use of herbs or using incantations to cast a spell on a person. I have direct reference to knowing our African roots or antecedents. We are, to be sure, an African people. Just as British, French, Italians, Germans, Asians, the Spanish surname, among others, take pride in their historical roots, we must dare to affirm our glorious African past. The African civilizations of Ghana, Melle, Songhai, Kanem-Bornu and Mossi states were in an advanced stage of civilization when Europe was in an inchoate or undeveloped state. We come from a past which soared far beyond the Edgar Rice Burroughs', "Tarzan" mythology of Black folk chasing a half-naked White man as he jumped from tree to tree. This invidious and dreadful portrayal is rank nonsense. Please read Chu and Skinner's *Glorious Age in Africa*, Lugar's *Tropical Africa*, Snowden's *Blacks in Ancient Antiquity*, Lerone Bennett's *They Came Before the Mayflower* and Ivan Van Sertima's *They Came Before Colum¬bus* in order to understand our right and variegated history

II. BELIEVE IN YOURSELF

I firmly believe that one of the principal reasons why so many of our young people are involved in alcoholism, substance abuse, Black on Black Crime, and "turf battles," among other manifestations of deviant behavior, is traceable to an immense absence of love and respect for self. The talented James Brown, as a result of his appealing and soulful rendition of "Say It Loud, I'm Black and I'm Proud," among other pulsating songs in the 1960's, was catapulted to national fame. The tragedy is that too many were simply saying the words without internalizing and believing in them.

I am convinced unless a person loves himself/herself, he/she will lack the capacity to love others. Conversely, I believe unless a person respects himself/herself, he/she will be unable to respect others. We as men must be about the process in our families and communities as active and visible affirmers of love and respect.

Always know that it only takes a few seconds to make a baby. However, it takes a man to care for his children and family.

III. SUPPORT HIGH EXPECTATIONS

The time has come to stop the perennial whining and complaining about what White people will or will not do for us. Correspondingly, we must cease and desist letting others define us as an endangered species. We are, in reality, what we believe we are. If we believe, as we must for our very survival and progress, that we can achieve, with opportunity, at the highest levels, then we will. Conversely, if we believe that we cannot achieve, then we will tend not to achieve.

While it is true that we suffer disproportionately in terms of unemployment and underemployment, wretched and inadequate housing, substandard health care and shoddy education, we, as a collective group, are not poor people. As Black citizens, we represent over $300 billion of our nation's Gross National Product. We must spend our disposable income in such a way as to have the dollar turn over more than once in our communities. It is not heretical to support Black businesses, schools and institutions of higher education. The message is simple THINK BIG, AND AIM HIGH.

IV. SOAR TO THE HEIGHTS

We are a people who have had to struggle, historically, "up the rough side of the mountain." In this conjunction, in spite of separate and unequal treatment and institutional and operational racism, we have fought with distinction in every war in which our nation has been. engaged. In point of fact the first person, Crispus Attucks, a Black man, was the first American to die for freedom on the Boston Commons on March 6, 1770. Over 5 000 Black persons fought in the Revolutionary War. We have fought, even when we did not enjoy freedom in behalf of human dignity and equality of opportunity the Revolutionary War to "Desert Storm."

The challenge for us 35 million Black citizens is to dare to keep faith with the Frederick Douglasses, Harriet Tubman, Sojourner Truths, Booker T. Washington, William E. B. Dubois's, Mary McCleod Bethune, Mordecai Wyatt Johnsons, Benjamin Mayses, Martin Luther Kings, Malcolm Xs, Rosa Parksese, Benjamin Hookses, Colin Powells, among a host of others, past and present, who urge us to push forward and upward. It is; indeed, time to soar Brothers, and I urge you, in this time and place, to soar like eagles for ourselves and our posterity.

Finally I should like to very briefly list 4 T's necessary for us to cohere maintain solidarity and keep faith with our remarkable past. The four Ts are as follows:

TENACITY

Dare to stick to the goals and objectives which will elevate and enrich There are too many Brothers who spend too much time talking about the "man" (reference to a White male) will permit us to do.. This, of course, is arrant nonsense, for we are men and must believe that we are! with opportunity, of doing what any other males, irrespective of race, do. Racism is a clear and present reality in our nation, but we must not permit ourselves to be paralyzed by racism. Our forebears were once in slavery, but never ceased believing and struggling for freedom. We struggled, as a people, in concert with fair-minded and human6 Whites to win passage of the Thirteenth Amendment in 1865 (abolished slavery in the United States), the Fourteenth Amendment in 1868 (conferred citizenship on former slaves), the Fifteenth Amendment in 1870 (provided Black males with the right Our collective struggle and sacrifice in recent history led to the passage of the 1957 Civil Rights Act, the 1960 Civil Rights Act, the 1964 Civil Rights Act, the 1965 Voting Rights Act and the 1968 Fair Housing Act. *We must continue to be tenacious in pursuing our dreams and aspirations.*

TOGETHERNESS

We must not allow ourselves to he divided by White racists or by Black Anglo-Saxons, interested in their own self-promotion and personal aggrandizement, to lead us into internecine warfare and divisive behavior. Our overarching concern must be what is in the best interest of the group and not the individual. Dare to practice "harambe" (i.e., togetherness) as we tackle socio-economic issues and the highest quality of education for our children and youths.

THOROUGHNESS

We must prepare ourselves through high quality education if we are to be competitive and effective in the American body politic. The global competition that our nation faces, especially against Japan and Germany, makes it imperative that ability and not race becomes the prime determinant as to who will achieve success in the workplace. Additionally, in ten years, a majority of the workers in the marketplace will be non-White Americans. We must be unremitting as we work with our children and within our communities in making certain that there are no viable substitutes for *truth and excellence*. Thoroughness in study and work habits will make a *happy and enduring difference*.

TEMERITY

I challenge you to be bold and risk-takers in support of a better nation and world for all. I offer two scriptural references for you to reflect on as you face life's challenges and opportunities: "The Lord is my light and my salva¬tion, whom shall I fear? The Lord is the strength of my life, of whom shall I be afraid?" (Psalms 27:1-2) In addition, "He has shown thee old man what is good and what doth the Lord require of thee, but to do justly, love mercy, and walk humbly with Thy God." (Micah6:8). We must embrace Imani (faith) and dare to step out on faith in support of human possibilities and a whole and an inclusive socio-racial body politic.

In conclusion, *"I Dare You to Care,* "maintain a strong and active spiri¬tual sense and affirm, in season and out, hope for a better tomorrow. Always know that "to whom much is given, much is required." Brothers, through it all, be strong, and *Sursum Corda* (Lift Up Your Hearts).

Let us, then, gird our hearts, fortify our minds and strengthen our society at war with itself. Let us step out intrepidly and courageously, believing firmly and unwaveringly:

"We are soldiers in the army. We have to fight although we have to cry. We have to hold up the bloodstained banner. We have to hold it up until we die."

It is we who must now hold high the torch of freedom and justice. Let us resolve, keeping faith with God, not to fail, and maintain the inextinguishable and luminous accomplishments, against fearsome societal odds, of our forebears. The mantle of leadership, responsibility and action has been passed to us. Let us *"Dare to Care"* and press forward to meet the wondrous challenges and opportunities of the present and the dawn of a new century. An unyielding faith in God and *Truth* and *Demonstrable Excellence*, as in times past, will surely set us free.

Presented to the Baltimore Branch, Association for the Study of Afro-American Life and History, Inc. - September 8, 1992

The Necessity of Black Colleges and Universities: A National Imperative

BACKGROUND

One of the tragic and lamentable realities of American history is that our nation was born with a fundamental hamartia (i.e., defect): SLAVERY. It, too, is calamitous and painful that 127 years after the formal end of slavery in the United States, as a result of the passage of the Thirteenth Amendment, the debilitating and injurious effects of slavery still remain in the United States. The passage of the Thirteenth (1865), Fourteenth (1868), and Fifteenth (1870) Amendments and subsequent civil rights legislation in contemporary times has not, except for *de jure* (i.e., by law), prevented the present socio-economic and economic institutional subordination of the overwhelm¬ing number of 35 million Black Americans in the American body politic. Black and White Americans continue to live in SEPARATE AND UNEQUAL WORLDS.

While Black citizens, to be sure, have made the historic and courageous leap from slavery to freedom, the preponderant number of Black citizens remains sequestered and far removed from the socio-economic, political and educational mainstream of our nation. This bleak and lugubrious situation prevails notwithstanding that we are the most powerful nation in the world with a Gross National Product in excess of five trillion dollars and over 108 million persons gainfully employed. In spite of the current recession, our nation is in a state of unprecedented prosperity.

The situation, however, for Black Americans, amidst the general affluence for White Americans, is dismal: unemployment for Black adults hovers around 14 percent; unemployment for Black youths is 45 percent; 48.7 percent of all Black children live in poverty; approximately 50 percent of Black children and youths entering the ninth grade in urban schools either drop out or are pushed out; Black citizens are disproportionately affected by the iniquitous effects of substance abuse, alcoholism, escalating teenage pregnancies, and expanding Black on Black crime; over 454,000 Black persons, primarily Black males, are in our nation's penal institutions; more Black males of college age (i.e.. 18-22) are in prison than in our nation's colleges and universities; over 15 million Black citizens are either poor or a part of the working poor. An understanding of these clear and painful realities, I believe, is essential to an understanding of the problems and opportunities which confront Black institutions of higher education.

CRISES CONFRONTING BLACK INSTITUTIONS OF HIGHER EDUCATION

The 117 historically Black institutions of higher education experience, to a substantial degree, the same socio-racial bifurcation and exclusion which beset 35 million Black Americans. It must be clearly understood that our nation has never made a firm commitment to equality of educational opportunity at any level (i.e., elementary through post-secondary education) for Black children and youths. This dreadful situation flows from an historic American ethos *vis-a-vis*.

Black persons:

(1) A pervasive belief that Black persons were not educable.

(2) A widespread belief that Black persons were genetically inferior to White persons.

In view of these two fallacious and egregious mythologies, no genuine effort was made to equalize educational facilities and to provide equality of opportunity for Black persons in our nation. Insofar as higher education was concerned, except for the passage of the Morrill Act in 1862 for the establishment of land-grant colleges in each state, there was no provision for any of the 500,000 Black person who were free. No provision was made for Black citizens until 28 years later with the passage of the so-called Second Morrill Act of 1890. As a result, a separate but unequal status, as was and is the case in elementary-secondary schools, was put in place for Black students. This situation remains the present *modus operandi* for Black students in majority Black institutions of higher education.

The primary problem confronting Black institutions of higher education today is the fact of grossly inadequate human and monetary resources to meet the needs of the 200,000 Black students currently enrolled in the 117 historically Black colleges and universities. Most Black students today, 800,000 in number, are enrolled in the 3,200 predominantly White institutions of higher education. The problems of insufficient human and monetary resources, Black "brain drain" to White institutions of higher education, too much remedial work, substandard facilities, among other pressing issues, must be addressed now. The problems which confront the 117 historically Black colleges and universities are not insoluble.

OPPORTUNITIES FOR BLACK INSTITUTIONS OF HIGHER EDUCATION

The chief opportunity which exists for historically Black colleges and universities is the education and development, as in times past, of Black youths for service and leadership. Black institutions are uniquely qualified and able to discharge this national mission. It is vitally important that Black youngsters in high school not be saturated with the view that they can, "Be All That You Can Be," only through the military. This misleading notion, to a large degree, accounts for a disproportionate number of Black men and women, over 25 percent, being in Saudi Arabia and the Persian Gulf during "Desert Storm." Black colleges and universities can be enormously helpful in providing Black students with the academic-technical knowledge and skills and confidence necessary for effective performance in a society dominated by cybernetics and high technology. Black colleges and universities, too, in the midst of an information age, can provide a spirit of caring, sharing and advocacy for the dispossessed and excluded. Moreover, a conduit for vertical mobility can be developed for the so-called permanent underclass.

CONCLUSION

There is an old Black Spiritual which states, in part, *"If I Ever Needed the Lord, I Need Him Now."* The same is decidedly true of our historically Black colleges and universities. We need our Black institutions of higher education to educate our young people for the demands, rigors challenges and opportunities of the Twenty-first Century. We as Black people in particular, through our financial gifts and lobbying efforts, must be in the forefront. The time to *"get on board"* in support of our historical Black institutions of higher education is at hand. Let us acquit ourselves through our actions and not through extravagant rhetoric and vein promises. Now is the time to begin, in earnest, to work in behalf of our very own-Black colleges and universities.

The Multicultural Debate:
How Do We Set Priorities

There is enormous ferment, trepidation and disquietude in our nation's public and private schools in regard to multicultural/multiethnic and multiracial instruction. This situation, to an overwhelming degree, represents a recrudescence of the push in the 1960's for pertinence and relevance in education as reflected in multicultural/multiethnic education. The primary difference today is that educators, parents, students and community groups, especially in public schools, are insisting upon greater depth and breadth in multicultural education.

Additionally, Black scholars such as Drs. Molefi Asante, Asa Billiard, James Banks, Ivan Sertima, among others, are emphasizing Afrocentric/multicultural education not only in history and social sciences but in all subjects. Dr. Molefi Asante, the nationally known chairperson of the African Studies Department at Temple University, is the chief proponent of Afro centricity, or Afro centric education. Dr. Asante's Afrocentric focus in education accentuates, within a multicultural perspective, a portrayal of history and the social sciences and related subjects from a Black or Afrocentric perspective. He does not, as has been erroneously reported, advocate a supplanting or extirpation of European history or Euro centricity (i.e., the teaching of history and the social sciences and related subjects from a White perspective).

The wide and heavy emphasis that our nation's media, electronic and print, has given to Afrocentric education as a vehicle for eliminating or supplanting Eurocentric education has led to obfuscation, consternation, misinformation, and recalcitrance to Afrocentric education as a vital and necessary part of multicultural education. The time, I believe, is now at hand to separate the chaff from the wheat and mythology from truth. Conferences of this type can be immeasurably helpful in defining terms and placing multicultural multiethnic education in a just and factual perspective.

The noted and highly revered historian, Arthur M. Schlesinger, Jr., almost apostatizes Hector St. John de Crevecoeur's romantic and illusory view of America as a "melting pot." He states:

> *He is an American, who, learning behind him all his ancient prejudices and manners, receives new ones from the new modes of life he has embraced, the new gov¬ernment he obeys, and the new rank he holds. The American is a new man who acts upon new principles . . . Here individuals of all nations are melted into a new race of men. (1)*

Schlesinger blithely sallies forth to support this monumental historical fallacy and hyperbole in proclaiming:

> *"E Pluribus Unum." The United States had a bril¬liant solution for the inherent fragility of a multiethnic society: the creation of a brand-new national identity., carried forward by individuals who, in forsaking old loyalties and joining to make new lives, melted away ethnic differences. (2)*

Andrew Hacker, in his insightful and potent Two Nations: Black and White Separate, Hostile and Unequal, portrays a continuing and deep-seated racial chasm in our nation:

> *Black Americans are Americans, yet they subsist as aliens in the only land they know. Other groups may remain outside the mainstream-some religious sects, for example: but they do so voluntarily, In contrast, Blacks must endure a segregation that is far from freely chosen. So America may be seen as two separate nations. Of course, there are places where the races mingle. Yet in most significant respects, the separation is pervasive and penetrating. As a social and human division, it surpasses all others—even gender— in intensity and subordination." (3)*

Hacker's observation, in reality, is an update or contemporary restate¬ment of the basic conclusion of the Kerner Report of 1968: ". . . two nations, separate, and unequal."

In a bleak concluding statement in Two Nations, Hacker offers a bleak and saturnine forecast for the future:

A huge chasm remains, and there are few signs that the coming
century will see it closed. A century and a quarter after slavery,
White America continues to ask of its Black citizens an extra
patience and perseverance that Whites have never required of
themselves. So the question for White Americans is essentially
moral: is it right to impose on members of an entire race a lesser
start in life, and then to expect from them a degree of resolution
that has never been demanded from your race? (4)

The impelling, pertinent and demanding issues raised by Schlesinger, Asante, Hilliard, John Henrico Clarke, Hacker, among others, must be addressed within a multicultural perspective. Afrocentric education is a vital and necessary component of multicultural education. Afrocentric education within a multicultural perspective constitutes a unifying, energizing and factual historical salad bowl. In short, the time is now at hand to begin a substantive and accurate de-mythologizing and de-mystification of Ameri¬can and world history to benefit all children and youths.

The late William Edward Burghardt DuBois, a towering scholar and prescient observer of American history and culture, offers a sanguine observation in the *Autobiography of W.E.B. DuBois:*

I know the United States. It is my country and the land of my
fathers. It is still a land of magnificent possibilities. It is still
the home of noble souls and generous people. But it is selling its
birthright. It is betraying its mighty destiny. I was born on its
soil and educated in its schools. I have never knowingly broken
its laws or unjustly attacked its reputation. At the same time, I
have pointed out its injustices and crimes and blamed it, rightly
as I believe, for its mistakes. It has given me an education and
some of its honors for which Iam thankful. (5)

Multicultural education, in terms of setting educational priorities, must be addressed in terms of axiological, ontological, and epistemological perspectives which accentuate social-racial and gender inclusiveness. We must not pursue the path of teaching the passive, hyperbolic and harmonistic dogmas of the past from whence cometh no truth.

1993

Truth and Service: Imperatives for the Present and Future

In this salubrious, radiant and inspirational setting, pregnant with hope, opportunity and promise, I take this opportunity to join with members of the entire "Sojourner-Douglass College Family in extending unlimited and joyous felicitations to the Sojourner-Douglass Class of 1993. Sagacity, persistence, drive, tenacity and a willingness to succeed, through it all, have led to the felicity and inimitable success which you richly savor and bask in today. , to be sure, have kept faith with the remarkable Sojourner Truth and redoubtable Frederick Douglass and countless others of our race who made "bricks without straw" and illumined the way for aficionados of freedom, socio-economic justice and demonstrable academic-intellectual excellence. We are most proud of you for keeping the dream of full freedom, wholeness and hum\n possibilities alive.

As you exult and rejoice with your relatives, friends, teachers and associates on this proud occasion, I believe, too, in my role as Commencement speaker, an obligation exists to challenge you to reflect on the past, ponder the present and plan/strategize for the future. The essence of this process requires making decisions or choices necessary for forward movement and progress. I am reminded of a potent observation made by Paul Robeson, one of the world's greatest artists, when he went to fight for Spain's freedom in 1938:

> *Every artist, every scientist, must decide now where he stands. He has no alternative. There is no standing above the conflict on Olympian heights. There are no impartial observers. Through the destruction, in certain countries, of the greatest of man's literary heritage, through the propagation of false ideas of racial and national superiority, the artist, the scientist, the writer is challenged. The struggles invade the formerly cloistered halls of our universities and other seats of learning. The battle-front is everywhere. There is no sheltered rear.*

Robeson concludes by asserting:

"The artist must elect to fight for Freedom or for Slavery. I had no alternative."

I wish it were possible to say to each of you today, resplendent in your academic regalia, filled with visions of a more tranquil and prosperous life and exuberant, after long and arduous study, about entering the world of letters that there were "sheltered rears" or a welcome surcease from "man's inhumanity to man." The bleak and stark reality is that such is not the case. Nonetheless, the distinctive and enduring work you have done here at your beloved Sojourner-Douglass College is far from being in vain, and you have every right to believe that better days loom ahead of you as you sally forth to meet the challenges of the 21st Century and beyond.

As you prepare to leave this venerable citadel of learning, please remember that she has rendered you a priceless and glorious terrestrial treasure— THE LIBERATION OF THE MIND. What you have learned here at Sojourner-Douglass College through hard work, struggle and a multiplicity of vicissitudes, frustration and pain, often not of your making, cannot be taken from you. The sum total of your academic-intellectual endeavor here has been directed toward ancient verities:

1. *THE POWER TO THINK FOR YOURSELF*
2. *SELF EMPOWERMENT AND LIBERA¬TION*
3. *THE ABILITY TO LOCATE NEEDED DATA OR SOURCES OF INFORMATION*
4. *THE ABILITY TO MAKE RATIONAL AND INFORMED DECISIONS*

These four elements will be enormously vital and consequential for you as you wrestle with three fundamental questions which have engaged hu¬mankind from the very beginning:

1. *Who Am I?*
2. *Where Am I Going?*
3. *How Do I Get There*

You owe a debt of gratitude to the administrators, staff and teachers who have provided a humane, caring and nurturing learning environment to enable you to be about the pulsating and exhilarating process of inquiry and the world of ideas.

As you enter the process of personal and collective academic-intellectual and civic involvement to improve the quality of life for all people, the imperishable and transcendent factors of TRUTH and SERVICE are crucial. The ancient Biblical admonition provides the necessary raison d'être or purpose for thought and action:

"To whom much is given, much is required."

What, then, are some of the challenges which, even in your tender years, will test your fettle and resolve? William Edward Burghardt DuBois, a titan in world letters, stated a towering problem for the world community in 1903:

"The problem of the Twentieth Century is the problem of the color line."

Tragically and lamentably, 90 years after DuBois' prophetic observation, the problem remains. In fact, in terms of an update, the problem of race may, too, be the problem of the Twenty-First Century.

Why we have made dizzying changes in moving from an agricultural society to an industrial-information age; made exciting medical breakthroughs as reflected in organ transplants and related medical advances, achieved the highest Gross National Product, over four trillion dollars, among other pioneer scientific, medical and industrial achievements, the world community still is not at peace with itself. The percentage of Blacks, Hispanics and the poor, in the richest nation in the world, continues to increase, the fratricidal war in Bosnia-Herzegovina continues, the majority Black South African population, under the tireless and extraordinary leadership of Nelson Mandela, inches painfully forward to freedom; the former Soviet Union has disintegrated; separate and unequal education remains thirty-nine years after *Brown vs. Board of Education of Topeka*, hunger, famine, drought and war engulf most underdeveloped countries in Africa and Asia; Somalia, Nigeria and Liberia, in particular, are torn by internecine conflict; socio-racial distinctions divide the world. The problems are manifold, complex and demanding

In stating a few of the vexatious and troubling conditions of the present, my point is not to make you peddlers of gloom and doom, but advocates and carriers of hope and believers in better tomorrows. You have what it takes to brighten the corner where you are. As you move forward, thinking for yourself, bear in mind that the greatest poems are yet to be written; our greatest medical and scientific breakthroughs are yet to come; more caring, resilient and imaginative teachers and administrators are yet to come; you possess the God-given talents and abilities to transform our society; racism, sexism, religious bigotry can be surmounted if we mobilize the will and work in earnest. In short, class of 1993, the best is truly before you through "TRUTH and SERVICE."

President William Jefferson Clinton, in his Inaugural Address, spoke of a new "Season of Hope and Opportunity." Fair and progressive Americans should rejoice in President Clinton's efforts for socio-racial and gender inclusiveness, even after his failure to support hapless and desperate Haitians and the debacle of Lani Guinier.

It, too, must be borne in mind that it is we, in the final analysis, which must save ourselves. In this spirit, I propose five non-negotiable imperatives:

1. *"Know your historical roots."* You come from strong stock and it is imperative that you mesh with it. In fact, you are the sum total of our historical roots, hopes, disappointments, intrepidity and aspirations and dreams for better tomorrows.

2. *"Cultivate and sustain a spiritual sense."* Men/Women need a spiritual anchor for human uplift and transcendent human possibilities and fulfillment.

3. *"Support and maintain love for family."* The family remains the essential leitmotif or linchpin for the progress of any society. Let the word go forth through you that "WE ARE FAMILY."

4. *"Believe in yourself with all your heart and mind."* One who truly believes in himself/herself will forswear drugs, deviant and assaultive behavior, self-hate and low self-concept, societal alienation and other forms of sociological and pathological maladies.

5. *"Be a risk-taker for freedom and socio-economic and educational equity and excellence."* Thinking and action will make these pursuits achievable and doable.

THE CENTRAL MESSAGE FOR EACH OF YOU: "CONTROL YOUR OWN MIND AND THINKING!'

I end as I began, with warmest congratulations to each of you for what you have accomplished here at Sojourner-Douglass College. As you leave, never forget that this community and Sojourner-Douglass will have need of you in the present and future.

Please remember the human condition is not immutable, but in a pro¬cess of evolving and change. Use your talents and abilities to enfeeble and extirpate racism, sexism, classism and religious bigotry.

Finally, in the euphoria which will follow the award of your hard-earned degree and later, in a more tranquil and contemplative period, ponder the five imperatives I submit as challenges and achievable human possibilities.

As you go forward and upward, be true to "TRUTH and SERVICE." The steadying, irrepressible, ineluctable, historic and sanguine promise remains:

> *Veritos vos liberatit ("And ye shall know the truth, and the truth shall set you free.") Class of 1993, Surslum Corda ("Lift up your hearts.")*
>
> *Congratulations and Godspeed in your career choices!*

New Journal & Guide - Norfolk, Virginia - November 24, 1993

Thanksgiving 1993: Time for Reflection and Action

Thanksgiving 1993 evokes memories of Charles Dickens' comment in terms of *"the best of times, the worst of times. We had everything before us, we had nothing before us."* It is demonstrably clear in our nation and the larger world community, that the Dickensian admonition is apt and fitting.

Thanksgiving, historically, has been a strong impetus for family gatherings, a rich and expansive fellowship, a contagious spirit of reverence and gratitude and a time of contemplation as we counted our blessings. The joy and happy contemplation of past Thanksgivings have been muted this year by the tragedies of the Haitian refugees, the fratricidal warfare in Bosnia-Heszegovina, the acrimony and bitterness depicted in the debates over the North American Free Trade Agreement (i.e. NAFTA), the Health Security Act and a general pervasiveness of "man's inhumanity to man" as shown in elevated crime levels, assaultive behavior, child abuse and mean-spiritedness.

Another troubling dimension as we prepare to observe Thanksgiving is the resurgence of racism, sexism and religious bigotry. *The larger white society which created the "socio-economic Frankenstein" re fuses to accept the clear and palpable reality of white racism.* There cannot and will not be fundamental social-economic justice, tranquility and endemic equality of opportunity until the larger white society "fesses up" or admits the pernicious, widespread and debilitating presence of white racism. *There is no such animal as Black racism because the elements of Control and Power are not available.*

A visit on Thanksgiving Day to such urban areas as New York, Philadelphia, Newark, New Jersey, Baltimore, Washington, D.C., Chicago, Detroit, among other areas, will reveal hordes of young destitute forlorn and alienated Black youth and adults with stolid, empty, haggard and hangdog expressions waiting for a cornucopia or the proverbial train of plenty to come. The train of hope and opportunity, to date, has left them bereft of sustenance and relief in an empty urban way station.

In spite of the growing pockets of bleakness and lost opportunities, I still believe that Black and poor people must dare to affirm Life, Hope and the Universal and Timeless Spirit of Thanksgiving. Each of us who has been blessed by God to have a measure of success, as a categorical and unconditional moral-ethical imperative, must help those who are "bone of our bone and flesh of our flesh."

We come from a historical tradition which, from "slavery to freedom," promoted and sustained caring, sharing an unbreakable spirit of "We are all in this together," love for ourselves and others, and high human possibilities. Once again, we have been summoned to answer the call, through service and assistance, to those who for a variety of reasons, have lost the way.

If we take this cardinal and urgent task seriously, I am very confident about the promise and possibilities for human uplift for Thanksgiving 1993 and beyond. It is in this spirit of hopeful anticipation that I say with firm conviction: Happy Thanksgiving, Brothers and Sisters.

1994

Afro-American - Baltimore, Maryland - April 27, 1994

Approaching Jubilation in South Africa

The persistent, resolute, sacrificial and unwavering efforts of black South Africans, after over 350 years of White domination and oppression, have begun to bear palpable and heartening results.

After long, tedious, complex and cumbersome negotiations, April 27, 1994, has been decided by President F. de Klerk for the election of a 400-member constituent assembly to draft a new constitution for South Africa.

While there are still pockets of recalcitrance, resistance, violence and anger within the majority White South African population, the "Freedom Train" is on the move in South Africa.

The work of the 400-member constituent assembly will be highly significant and pivotal in terms of what form the new government will take.

There is much talk by de Klerk and some White South African leaders of the development of a governmental structure which supports proportional representation.

The African National Congress, led superbly by Nelson Mandela and Cyril Ramaphsa, general secretary of the ANC, are wedded to majority Black representation.

In view of the fact that Black South Africans represent 85 percent of the electorate, it will be difficult for them to support the principle of broad-based or proportional White representation. Majority Black representation represents a fair, just and inescapable political reality.

Majority Black South African participation is moving forward inexorably and precisely because over 25 million Black South Africans never lost sight of the prize of full freedom, social justice and dignity.

Moreover, in the face of internal and external ploys and maneuvers to cause friction, strife and violence between and among the members of the

African National Congress, led by Nelson Mandela and Chief Mangosuthu Buthelizi, leader of the Inkatha Party, an overwhelming majority of Black South Africans stayed the course in support of unity and solidarity.

The South African population, under the atavistic, brutal, dehumanizing and horrendous practice of apartheid, has paid a high price in terms of lives lost in the struggle, illegal imprisonments and torture, and denial of elemental human and civil rights.

Nonetheless, under the courageous leadership of such Black South African leaders as Nelson and Winne Mandela, Walter Sisulu, Bishop Tutu, Allan Boesak, Cyril Ramaphosa, among others, a firm, realistic and achievable process for majority Black controls and power is now in place.

The just, implacable, and egalitarian demands of the Black South African population have set the stage for power-sharing, social justice and the dawn of a new era in South African history.

Lovers of freedom, throughout the world community, have every right to rejoice and be glad as freedom, belatedly, evolves in South Africa.

The Baltimore Sun - November 3, 1994

I Q Book Condemned for Racism

Upon reading the late Richard J. Hernstein's and Charles Murray's *"The Bell Curve: Intelligence and Class Structure in American Life."* I felt a keen sense of incredulity and disquieting déjà vu.

The authors, in their tendentious, voluminous and mean-spirited 806-page tome, continue, in elegant and mellifluous language, to set forth a proposition that Black citizens as a group are less intelligent than White citizens.

In essence, Messrs. Hernstein and Murray set forth a chimerical and virulent racist agenda.

Their book bespeaks an effort made by Arthur Jensen's How Much Can We Boost I. Q. 's and by Edward Banfield and William Shockley in the 1960's, 1970's and 1980's to portray Black citizens as inferior to White citizens in the American politic.

Those noxious, venal and racist theories were thoroughly repudiated by most scholars and academics and consigned to a fitting repose, the scrap heap.

There are, to be sure, serious flaws in the *Bell Curve.*

Individuals are judged/evaluated as individuals and not as a group. There are individuals within the groups who achieved very favorably on cognitive measurements, but they are not, as a matter of accuracy, classified as a group.

The reality is that most of the 5.7 billion people who comprise our world are average. High and low achievement levels occur among individuals in all ethnic-racial populations.

The audacious and iconoclastic posturing of the authors breaks no new ground in the areas of genetics, intelligence testing and psychometrics.

The central motif of their book, void of panegyrics and arcane language, is to show the fundamental inferiority of Black people. The same pseudo and self-serving arguments were used in the 18th century by Thomas Jefferson, Thomas Dew of William and Mary College, and others.

The authors roundly excoriate and denounce what they call an "ideology of equality." One wonders where over 250 million persons in our nation would be if the promise of equality of opportunity and a fair chance had not been available to them.

In spite of 204 years of slavery and over a century (1865-1994) of institutional and operational racism experienced by Black citizens, past and present, the authors fail to address this clear and present political, socio-economic and educational burden.

The Bell Curve has attracted enormous attention in the national media because of an endemic spirit of retreat, retrenchment, and indifference to civil and human rights. The time, in short, is propitious for their racist, divisive and demeaning tract.

I believe, however, that citizens of rationality and fundamental decency and fairness will see through the racist appeal of *The Bell Curve.*

I believe it is in our national interest to rise above the denigration and subordination of any group because of race, gender, religion or ethnic background.

1995

The New Majority: Implications for Higher Education

The Republicans' triumph on Tuesday, November 8, 1994, provided clear and palpable evidence of a new majority in the Congress and an intensification and expansion of socio-racial bifurcation and estrangement in the American body politic. *The fundamental and stark realities of the Republicans' victory on November 8, 1994, and their concomitant call for a "Contract with America" constitute an affirmation of national meanness and racism. No group will be immune to or beyond the purview of the Republicans' national effort, through their "Contract with America," to redirect, restructure and modify the socio-economic, educational and political direction of our nation.*

It is demonstrably clear that the Republicans' victory has direct and substantive implications for over 3,300 institutions which constitute the network of higher education in our nation. The central breakdown, I believe, as in times past, will be along socio-racial lines. While it is true that most institutions will be challenged economically, given programs of fiscal austerity, attenuated human and monetary resources and a dwindling pool of students able to attend college, the 117 historically Black colleges and universities will be sorely pressed. The historic, persistent and endemic factors of race and class remain a heavy, onerous and debilitating onus for historical Black colleges and universities (i.e., HBCUs). *In view of the historic exclusion of historically Black colleges and universities from the socio-economic and educational mainstream of our nation, this paper, in addressing the implications of "THE NEW MAJORITY" in higher education will focus primarily on historically Black colleges and universities because they are at greater risk and in a tenuous and sorely uneven position.*

In this conjunction, Black persons have historically been denied the opportunity for equal educational opportunity in elementary-secondary schools and institutions of higher education in our nation. During the period of slavery (i.e., 1661-1865), there was almost a universal *Zeitgeist* or spirit of the times that affirmed the view of Black persons as a suborder of life and that their "small brains" could not endure the rigors of education. Thomas

Jefferson, the third president of the United States and "sage of Monticello, spoke confidently and forthrightly about Black persons:

> *Comparing them (i.e., slaves) by their faculties of memory, reason, and imagination, it appears to me, that in memory they are equal to Whites; in reason much inferior, as I think one could scarcely be found capable of tracing and comprehending the investigation of Euclid... .In imagination they are dull, tasteless and anomalous.(1)*

Almost as an afterthought, Jefferson would express the natural rhythm theme associated with Black persons: "In music they are more generally gifted than the Whites with accurate ears for tune and time...(2)"

The racist, spurious and debasing comments of Jefferson, among others (Thomas Dew, John C. Calhoun) set in place a psychological and national imprimatur mindset before and after the Civil War which placed Black persons in a position of institutional subordination and exclusion. *This process continues today under different disguises and forms.*

The racist pronouncements of Jefferson, Thomas Dew and John C. Calhoun. Among others, gave encouragement and emboldened self-appointed authorities of the alleged educational, intellectual and cognitive deficits of Black persons to sally forth. Senator Ben "Pitchfork" Tillman of South Caro¬lina would deliver a virulent and acrimonious attack in the U.S. Senate at the dawn of the 20th century: "We have done our best (i.e., disenfranchisement of Black voters in South Carolina). We have scratched our heads to find out how we could eliminate the last one of them. We stuffed ballot boxes. We shot them. We are not ashamed of it." (3)

Congressman John Sharp Williams, speaking at an earlier time, would intensify the scurrilous attacks on Black persons in an effort to portray their basic inferiority. Williams, in a caustic and invidious address on December 20, 1898, would declare;

> *You could shipwreck 10,000 illiterate White Americans on a desert island, and in three weeks they would have a fairly good government, conceived and administered upon fairly democratic lives. You could shipwreck 10,000 Negroes, every one of whom was a graduate of Harvard University, and in less than three years, they would have retrograded governmentally; half of the*

men would have been killed, and the other half would have two wives apiece. (4)

Lastly, Senator James K. Vardaman, speaking in the United States Senate, spoke obstreperously and vitriolic ally:

Mr. President, I am not the Negro's enemy. I know what is best for him. I think I can measure his productive capacity. I know the influences that move him. I am familiar with the currents which sweep through his savage blood. I think I know him as he really is. The pure-blooded Negro reaches mental maturity as soon as he passes the period of puberty. The cranial sutures become ossified by the time he reaches 20 years of age and it is not uncommon to find one who reads fluently at 15 years of age and not to know a letter in the book at the age of 25 or 30. (5)

It is, to be sure, no intent to offer an abbreviated historical exegesis on racist thought, predilections and proclivities, past and present, but to provide a level of insight and understanding of venomous thoughts and actions which have kept Black HCBUs and Black people in general in a position of socio-economic and educational marginality and exclusion from the center of power in the American body politic.

The same racial duality and "two-ness" which Black persons have endured since the establishment of land-grant colleges in the United States remains, to a substantial degree, in effect today. The passage of the Morrell Act in 1862 provided a legal basis for the establishment of land-grant colleges for Black persons. It is ironic, in principle, at least, "the nation, six years before the Plessy vs. Ferguson decision, was making an effort to provide 'separate but unequal' education in the institutions of higher education." (6)

The plan of the Republicans, as set forth in their Contract with America, will, if enacted, continue a socio-racial dichotomy in America's institutions of higher education and American life in general. The plan to eliminate $45 billion, over a five-year period, in socio-economic programs of uplift and growth will constitute another barrier and burden to 32 million Black Americans who have been denied equity and excellence in the American social order. Once again, Black Americans will be called upon to make bricks without straw. *A disproportionate number of Black students who came from poor or marginal families will find less money available in terms of loans and grants.* A concentrated effort, too, will be made by the Republican majority to eliminate or curtail Head Start, free lunch and breakfast programs; the Women, Infants and Children (child-nutrition program) money for crime prevention and Aid to Families with Dependent Children (i.e., welfare or public assistance). A curtailment or evisceration of programs of this type will contribute significantly to a socio-racial chasm in the American social order.

As I have indicated, I believe the road ahead will be very difficult, taxing and cumbersome for historically Black colleges and universities and Black people in general. The publication of Richard Herrnstein's and Charles Murray's *The Bell Curve; Intelligence and Class Structure in American Life* provides a recrudescence of the fallacious and specious and mythological arguments of such persons as Thomas Jefferson, Thomas Dew, John C. Calhoun, Arthur Jensen, William Shockley, and Edward Banfield to depict the basic inferiority of Black people. *The Atlanta Constitution*, in a lead editorial entitled, "Race and IQ Tests," on October 14, 1994, stated in regard to *The Bell Curve*, "The authors of *The Bell Curve* pose as brave intellectual rebels, but there is little that is brave or rebellious about stomping on the disadvantaged and pandering to the powerful. There is a long and discredited tradition of racists trying to cloak their prejudice in pseudoscience." (7)

Robert J. Samuelson in an op-ed column which appeared in the *Washington Post* on October 26, 1994 on The Bell Curve entitled *"Bell Curve Ballistics"* stated:

> *Although Charles Murray is no bigot, The Bell Curve does invite misuse. The book can rationalize racism and fatalism in both Whites and Blacks. It is a pretext for both Whites and Blacks to think the worst of each other. And it is a ready-made excuse for both to lapse into personal and political passivity on the grounds that nothing can be done. In this sense, The Bell Curve and the violent reactions to it are, as much as anything else, a commentary on America's present pessimism. (8)*

Herrnstein's and Murray's *The Bell Curve* has sold over 200,000 copies and remains in enormous demand. The book's exaltation of the "cognitive elite," determined by genes and viewed as immutable, and condemnation of what they call an "ideology of equality received a very favorable response in the larger White society. Herrnstein and Murray, too, seek, in pragmatic terms or real politic, to provide a raison d'être or validation of the preferred status of White citizens based upon, as a group, a 15-point cognitive deficit of Black citizens because of "inferior" genes. *This position is put forth notwithstanding their mea culpa that an individual should not be judged as a member of a group but as an individual. In reality, The Bell Curve, shows euphemisms, circumlocutions and archaic language, and is a paean to institutional racism and exclusivity. No attention is given to the deleterious effects that racism and injurious and egregious environmental factors have had past and present, on Blacks, Hispanics, Native Americans, and the poor.*

WHAT MUST BE DONE TO ENHANCE BLACK AND POOR PEOPLE AND HISTORICALLY BLACK COLLEGES AND UNIVERSITIES?

As vehement and sophisticated attacks are waged on affirmative action, public assistance, equal job opportunities, fair housing, equity and excellence in elementary-secondary schooling and higher education and affordable health care for all Americans, it is abundantly clear that our nation is moving in the direction of a national triage: WHO CAN OR SHOULD BE HELPED OR SAVED? At the end of World War II, the National Servicemen's Readjustment Act ("G.I. Bill") was established which resulted in over 7 million former members of the armed forces having the benefit of higher education and decent, safe and affordable housing. This group now constitutes middle-and upper-class America. Additionally, after the former Soviet Union bedazzled the world by placing Sputnik into orbit in March 1957, our nation mobilized the resources to place a team on the moon and shored up teaching in mathematics and science. Other subjects were added, through the establishment of national seminars, workshop and instruction in institutions of higher education under the aegis of the National Defense Education Act.

The same sense of national urgency which was generated for former GI's and upgraded instruction in mathematics and science and other subject areas (viz., history, English, etc.) must now be set in place to strengthen institutions of higher education; especially historically Black colleges and universities, and to improve the quality of life for 258 million citizens in the American social order. Current efforts like Proposition 1817 in California, now on hold through a court injunction, and an embryonic effort by Thomas Wood and Glynn Custard, proponents of what they call the "Civil Rights Initiative" in California to outlaw affirmative action through legislative action in 1996, must be resisted as contrary to fundamental justice and equality of opportunity.

The emergence of the so-called "New Majority" must not be an occasion for perpetual lamentations, sack-cloth and ashes and a WOE IS ME mentality as we endeavor to make real the promise of equity and excellence for all students. The ascension to power of Newt Gingrich as Speaker of the House, Bob Dole as the Senate Majority Leader, Jesse Helms as chairperson of the Foreign Relations Committee and Orrin Hatch as chairperson of the Senate Judiciary Committee, among other Republican appointments, represents tangible evidence that belt-tightening will be the watchword for institutions of higher education and HBCUs in particular. Additionally, equality of opportunity and social justice will not be on the national front-burner. Nonetheless, I believe, as in our not too distant past, we must continue to press forward through the judicious use of the ballot, non-violent protests and public pronouncements to prevent an unconscionable and immedicable retreat or transmogrification or a burlesque of elemental freedom for all Americans. *Institutions of higher education as the citadels for truth and excellence must be in the forefront for fundamental freedom, truth and equity for all.*

Finally, in terms of *The Bell Curve,* which serves as a political tract for the "New Majority's" political propensities, I believe it is imperative, as a matter of academic intellectual honesty, integrity and essential fairness, that Black and White scholars and lay people respond with truth, accuracy and determination. There must not be a conspiracy of silence that emerged with Adolph Hitler's *Mein Kampf,* and the subsequent annihilation of 11 million people, 6 million of whom were Jews, and his maniacal efforts for world domination based upon a fictional "master race." While it is true that Herrnstein and Murray do not speak of a "master race," they do posit the proposition of a "cognitive elite." What then, will be done with those who are not a part of the "cognitive elite?" *The Hitlerian modality for "final solution" was enforced sterilization and genocide for "undesirables."*

In the final analysis, all institutions of higher education, keeping faith with their genesis and *raison d'être,* must dare, through it all, to affirm the ancient biblical admonition: *VERITAS, vos liberatit-"Ye shall know the truth and the truth shall set you free."* The time, I believe, is now at hand, without fear or favor, for us to go forward, in this proud and purposeful and liberating spirit, for high, enduring and irrepressible human and academic-intellectual possibilities.

Dare to Use the Power of Education to Soar to the Heights

As we meet today, I have chosen to address the topic, *"Dare to Use the Power of Education to soar to the Heights."* It is vitally important to know that education is power only when it is put to use. The administration, faculty, staff, parents and alumni/alumnae associated with this venerable institution can be enormously helpful to you as you transform the human condition.

> *It is equally important for each of you to know that a time existed here at "Poly"and throughout the Baltimore City Public Schools, not withstanding your abil¬ity, interest and academic-intellectual attainments, because of school segregation, based on color, you could not attend Poly or other so-called White schools until legal pressure was brought by the Baltimore Branch, NAACP, with the late Thurgood Marshall serving as legal counsel, to have students admitted to Poly and later to other formerly all-White schools.*

Baltimore City's Board of School Commissioners, in an historic action, permitted 17 carefully screened Black male students to enter Poly in September, 1952. This historic action took place two years before segregation was officially ended in the Baltimore City Public Schools by the *Brown* decision of May 17, 1954. Baltimore decided to voluntarily end *de jure* segregation (i.e., by law) in September, 1952.

The remarkable resolve, fortitude, courage, pluck and academic-intellectual staying power of the 17 Black students, *"the Poly 17"*, served as the basis for the desegregation of venerable Poly in 1952. Each of you, mindful of the *"Poly 17"* and others, who have followed, has a glorious, inspirational and indelible academic tradition to follow and uphold. I am confident that you will be equal to the task because of your knowledge of your heritage, the high expectations for each of you, the solid support of your administrators, teachers and parents and your desire to be a *WINNER. We are counting on you!*

Poly, to be sure, is richer and stronger as a result of the admission of female students in 1978. Gender segregation was also ended at City College Senior High School and Eastern High School. As I look at this audience this morning, I see evidence of female-male enthusiasm, expectancy and comeliness. The end of racial segregation in the Baltimore City Public Schools in September, 1952, heralded the end of gender segregation.

A review of the 261 million persons in our nation shows that all had valuable and distinctive antecedents as expressed in coming from Europe, Africa, Asia and other parts of the world community. The only indigenous people in America were the Native Americans.

Black History Month celebrates the history, life and contributions of Black Americans in national and world history. In this historic sense, 32 million Black persons in our nation came form Mother Africa. Long before Europe and developed African states such as Ghana, Songhai, Mille, Kanem-Bornu, the Mossi States, among others, were flourishing and advanced civilizations. Early African states took the lead in the smelting of iron, domesticating of animals, developing forms of government and establishing world renowned institutions of higher education. This period, long before the arrival of the Portuguese in 1441, was a glorious and proud period in African history. *This remarkable history needs to be shared by all persons.*

The cruel and deadly African slave trade, called the "Triangle Trade," resulted in approximately 40 million Africans perishing between 1450 to 1865. Through it all, the love of freedom, pluck and sheer grit and determination enabled Black people to persevere and pass the torch to future generations. You, in your tender years, are a special and vital part of this tradition.

You, too, are a bright and valued part of our forebears, who, in spite of dreadful trials and tribulations, dared, through an unflinching faith in God and persistence, made the leap from slavery to freedom in 1865.

I wish it were possible, as I recount the bold leap of faith of our forebears, that I could say to you in honesty that racism, sexism and religious bigotry did not exist. A major challenge for you will be to use the knowledge and insights you acquire here at Poly to press forward and upward. *The highest quality of education will be necessary in order for you to hold the torch of freedom, excellence and human dignity.* Education is power and it is an invincible or unbeatable force in the age-old struggle against "man's inhumanity to man." Then, too, remember that excellence, in reality, is "colorless." Excellence is not Black, White, Red, Brown, male, female, but a sparkling and irrepressible UNIVERSAL. I CHALLENGE YOU, IN YOUR TENDER YEARS, HERE AT POLY, TO SEIZE AND HOLD EXCELLENCE.

The second challenge I pose for you is to BELIEVE IN YOURSELF. A genuine belief in self, too, imposes a love and respect for others. *"If you do not love and respect yourself, you will not be able to love and respect others."* An abiding love and respect for self, in your adventuresome, exciting and terribly curious youth, will enable you to forswear or forsake alcohol, sub¬stance abuse, promiscuous sexual activity and a self-defeating *"GET-BY"* attitude in your classes and life in general.

Education can help you to see "worlds" unknown to you now. Education can help you to become liberated and empowered in the marvelous and invigorating world of ideas. I have posed for your reflection and thought two principle challenges for Black History Month and beyond: (1) *Know your historical roots and take pride in yourself;* (2) *Love and respect ourselves and others irrespective of race, color, class and gender.*

We are an African people, and we deserve to be proud of this fact. However, it is very important that we share our rich history with all who make up the human family.

Always remember that a lighted torch of freedom, hope, dignity and pride has been passed on to you from Africa to America. Kings and queens of the African experience and stalwarts such as Gabriel Prosser, Denmark Vesey, Nat Turner, Sojourner Truth, Harriet Tubman, Frederick Douglass, Booker T. Washington, Dr. William Edward Burghardt DuBois. Dr. Martin Luther King, Jr., Malcolm X, and an army of others, are saying to you even now: *"Keepers of the torch, and we are counting on you!"* Education is your passport to a better life and the means to *"Soar to the Heights!"* I challenge you, in your restless and daring, full of promise, to seize education and use it wisely.

In the mid-nineteenth century, David Walker, a fearless, brave and self-taught Black man, made a powerful statement that I leave as a final challenge to you, spirited and highly able keepers of the torch, of "FREEDOM AND EXCELLENCE: "I would crawl on my hands and knees through mud and mire, to the feet of a learned man, where I would humbly supplicate him to instill in me, that which neither devils nor tyrants could remove, and with my life— for colored people to acquire learning in this country, makes tyrants quake and tremble on their sandy foundations." Young men and women of

Poly, go forward and upward with education as your shield and guide for "TRUTH, EXCELLENCE AND EMPOWERMENT."

There are those, even now, who will say to many of you, as we have recently witnessed at Rutgers University, that you cannot achieve because of "genetic hereditary" deficits or weaknesses. One of the most effective ways you can counteract such racist thought as students is when people say you can't do because of your race or color, "SIMPLY DO! DO PHYSICS, CHEMISTRY, ALGEBRA, AND GEOMETRY. TRIGONOMETRY; SPEAK in Standard English in all of your classes: be ANALYTICAL in history and other subject offerings. In short, "LET YOUR MIND SPEAK" for you when others talk about what they believe or perceive you can't do. You are a" WATU WAZURI" (Beautiful People), and in your tender years, we are counting on you to make a "HAPPY DIFFERENCE" in a world at war with itself.

Presented to the Brown Bag Lecture Series, Sponsored by the
Mayor of Baltimore City and the Baltimore Community
Relations Commission. February 16, 1995

Black Americans at the Edge of the Educational Precipice: Challenges and Opportunities

In 1903, in his classic, *The Souls of Black Folk*, Dr. William Edward Burghardt DuBois, historian-educator extraordinaire, stated prophetically and accurately: "The problem of the twentieth century is the problem of the color line." It is lamentable and disquieting, to be sure, that 90 years later, the ancient color line continues to bedevil, frustrate and divide us as a nation.

No group, with the exception of Native American, in the American body politic, has suffered more than 32 million Black citizens. The color line has consigned the preponderant number of Black citizens to the bottom of the socio-economic and educational totem pole. This situation is painfully, viscerally and palpably evident in our nation's network of 15,764 school districts serving 40 million students and the network of 3,200 institutions of higher education with a clientele in excess of 12 million students.

The primary focus of my remarks today centers on elementary-secondary schooling. It should be noted, at the very outset, that our nation has never, in truth and deeds, made a firm, unflagging and unequivocal commitment to equity and fairness in public education. Black students in both elementary-secondary education and higher education are in a tertiary or *separate but unequal status* notwithstanding the historic and momentous *Brown vs. Board of Education of Topeka* decision of May 17, 1954 and subsequent Federal and legislative actions in support of equality of educational opportunity.

> *Over 8 million Black students in our nation's public schools tend to be at the lower educational strata and are in a precarious and marginal educational position and the beneficiaries, overwhelmingly of shoddy and ineffectual education because of a genuine lack of a demonstrable commitment to equality of opportunity and excellence for all. It is this malodorous, vexatious and lamentable reality which has placed Black students, at all levels (i.e., elementary-secondary and higher*

*educational), teetering and excluded from the socio-economic
and political mainstream of our nations.*

When the U.S. Supreme Court decided unanimously, after two years
of protracted litigation, that segregation in our nation's public schools
was unconstitutional, there was pervasive and unrestrained jubilation and
euphoria among Black Americans. The reaction, at first, among most White
Americans, was a brooding cynicism, uneasiness and anger. However, when
the Supreme Court, in what is now commonly referred to as *Brown II,*
which was declared on Monday, May 31, 1955, ruled that school districts
should proceed *"with all deliberate speed"* to dismantle segregated schools, a
mood and action of obfuscation, recalcitrance, violence and school closing
enveloped most segregated school districts. *The Baltimore City Public School
district, to its immense credit, agreed to desegregate its schools in September,
1954.* It too is significant that an anomaly developed in Baltimore, prior to
the May 17, 1954, Brown decision, that the Baltimore City Board of School
Commissioners agreed to permit 17 carefully selected Black students to enter
Baltimore Polytechnic's "A Course" in September, 1952. All other schools
remained segregated until the Brown decision of May 17, 1954.

Throughout the South, official positions of delay and resistance to Brown
as expressed in "interposition," nullification, obfuscation, intimidation and
violence prevented Black youngsters from enjoying equality of educational
opportunity. Virginia shut down the Prince Edward County Public schools
for five years (i.e., 1959-1964) and school districts in other parts (viz., Norfolk,
Front Royal, and Charlottesville) of the Old Dominion for much shorter
periods. The "Little Rock Nine," as a result of the defiance and meretricious
behavior of Governor Orval Faubus, had to be escorted to Little Rock's
Central High School by Federal troops in 1957. Only Ernest Green was able
to complete his schooling and to be graduated from Central High School.

While it is true that *de facto* (i.e., in practice) segregation obtains, to
a substantial degree, in our nation's public schools. Black students largely
sequestered or concentrated in large urban, segregated school districts, North
and South have been denied fundamental equity and fairness in our nation.

A basic lack of commitment by our national and state leaders, woefully
inadequate human and monetary resources, and a troubling and stereotypical
belief that Black youngsters have cognitive deficits have contributed to
substandard educational opportunity for the vast majority of over 8 million

Black youngsters in our nation's public schools. <u>This situation is calamitous and unconscionable</u> 40 years after the <u>Brown</u> decision.

It is equally painful and troubling that President Francis Lawrence of Rutgers has not only denigrated and impugned the Black students matriculating at Rutgers by referring to their deficient "generic, hereditary background," but in essence Black people throughout our nation. Dr. Lawrence's comments, in truth, are an attempt to validate, in genteel and euphemistical language, the arrant and unmitigated racism contained in Richard Herrnstein's and Charles Murray's, *The Bell Curve: Intelligence and Class Structure in American Life.* Dr. Lawrence has forfeited the moral authority and leadership necessary for Rutgers' cohesion and solidarity and should, in my firm belief, resign the presidency of Rutgers forthwith.

It should be noted that in Baltimore, primarily through the vision, sagacity, perseverance and indefatigable efforts of Mayor Kurt L. Schmoke, even in the midst of grossly attenuated and scarce human and monetary capital, education has been made the centerpiece of the Schmoke administration. It is hoped that other political leaders will follow Mayor Schmoke's example in making education a priority through deeds and demonstrable example.

As we meet here today, in this salubrious, sanguine and majestic setting, it is most important to recall that 40 percent of Black youngsters who enter the ninth grade will fail to graduate; 42.7 percent of children under 18 in our nation live in abject poverty; unemployment among Black youths ap¬proximates 40 percent in large urban centers; Black youths and adults com¬prise 40 percent of the 1.1 million persons in our nation's penal institutions; approximately 18 million Black adults are in poverty or a part of the working poor; unemployment among Black adults hovers around 11 percent; over 14 million Black citizens are sequestered in substandard, unsanitary and wretched housing and lack health care or medical insurance. Over eight million Black children served by our nation's public schools are a part of this parlous, tragic and debilitating matrix. They are at risk not because they lack academic-intellectual ability, but because our nation has doggedly and persistently refused, past and present, to make a commitment, in a holistic or comprehensive way, to them and their parents' and grandparents' well-being, progress, prosperity and socio-economic wholeness.

In spite of this Draconian, dreadful and deadly situation, I believe there remains a basis for HOPE, HUMAN RENEWAL AND RECONCILIATION. Unlike pre-Brown or the period before May 17, 1954, when the official policy of our nation sanctioned and supported segregation in our national life, our government today, in spite of the socio-economic and educational problems, has placed its official imprimatur on equality of opportunity for all citizens. As a people who made the historic and fitful leap from slavery to freedom, we must take full advantage of our constitutional rights and opportunities. To this end, we must work assiduously, tenaciously and unflinchingly, as a people who have historically possessed a burning passion for freedom, social justice and educational excellence and to do whatever is legitimate and morally just and right to prevent the educational destruction of another generation of Black children and youths. Freedom, demonstrable excellence and social justice for all must be non-negotiable and placed on our nation's front burner.

We have lost several generations of Black youngsters since the Brown decisions of Monday, May 17, 1954, and Monday, May 31, 1955. As we prepare to enter the Twenty-first century, accentuating the "information age" and cybernetics (i.e., high technology), we must muster the will, courage and resources to transcend, *in the national interest*, the ancient foes of racism, sexism and religious bigotry. *A person's color, race, religion, social standing or gender must not be the primary determinant as to whether he/she achieves success and fulfillment in the American social order.*

Finally, we must dare to respond clearly and affirmatively to two elemental questions as we come to grips with an emerging *educational triage*: (1) *who shall be saved?* (2) *Whom do you wish to save?* It is, I believe, essential for our nation's unity, prosperity and stability, to affirm, through deeds, our BEST must be provided for all. All children and youths, irrespective of color, gender, social class and ethnicity, must have a chance to succeed.

The under-utilization and dissipation of this nation's most precious resource, its children and youths, can no longer be deferred because some of them were not born White. Our nation possesses abundant human and monetary resources to assure genuine educational opportunity for all of its citizens. It must now muster the will and resources. *Now*, at a late juncture in our nation's history, is the time to begin anew and in earnest.

Excellence in Education: A Costly Proposition

Public education, historically, has played a vital, pivotal and prominent role in the development, growth and posterity of our nation. Our nation, even before the national establishment of public schools for all following the Civil War in 1865, has made public education a prized possession and the sine qua non necessary for societal cohesion, unity and an informed citizenry.

In support of this proposition, Horace Mann, a formidable, prescient and seminal leader in the struggle for free public schools in America well over a century ago, viewed education as the "equalizer of the condition of men." (1) The potential exists today for education to be the great "equalizer" for boys and girls and men and women. What is urgently needed is "a mobilization of will, resources and commitment." (2)

The central motif or emphasis of this paper is stated directly: The under-utilization and dissipation of our nation's most precious resource, it's children and youths, can no longer be deferred because some of them were not born White. Our nation possesses abundant human capital and monetary resources to ensure genuine equality of educational opportunity for all of its citizens. It must now, at a late date, muster the will and resources. Now, at a very late juncture in our nation's history, is the time to begin anew and in earnest.

Education, to an overwhelming degree, in the development and growth of our nation, has served as a socio-economic and political escalator. In point of fact, from the time of the founding of the Boston Latin Grammar School in 1635 and Harvard in 1636, the civic and social elites and leadership have come from the recipients of high quality education. This situation has tended to remain true with the establishment of a sound and expansive system of public education after 1865, and the forward momentum, with wider racial and gender inclusiveness, in contemporary times.

However, it should be noted that a major encumbrance or hamartia (i.e., youths equality of educational opportunity until the momentous *Brown vs. Board of Education* decision of May 17, 1954. The *Brown* decision toppled the

Plessy vs. Ferguson decision of 1896, which ushered in legal segregation in our national life. The *Plessy* decision, which, ironically, involved a transportation case in New Orleans, resulted in the national government placing its official imprimatur on official segregation in all aspects of our national life with the principle of "separate but equal." Our nation has paid an enormous societal price in terms of the *Plessy* decision as reflected in the prodigal and extravagant operation of dual school systems in the various states, disunity, distrust, and lack of high academic performance for all students.

While it is true that *de jure* segregation has ended, the clear and present reality of *de facto* segregation remains a monumental and demanding challenge for our nation as regards equal educational access, opportunity and equity for all children and youths. Race and class must not be allowed to be the chief determinants for educational opportunity and excellence in the American body politic. It is highly significant that you, as the policy makers for schools in Eastern Virginia, have come together to explore, examine and implement techniques, strategies, policy formulations and paradigms which will support racial, gender and socio-economic inclusiveness and demonstrable excellence for all children and youths.

A decade ago, the National Commission on Excellence, in its highly heralded and acclaimed report, warned of a "rising tide of mediocrity afflicting our nation's public schools. The basic catalyst for the urgency of the report was the fact of declining Scholastic Aptitude Test results for White students. Black students and other non-White minority students were treated in the report in a very marginal or tertiary manner. There have been over twenty-five major reports focusing on the need for school reform since the National Commission's report. Except for John Goodlad's *A Place Called School*, Theodore Sizer's *Horace's Dilemma and the Quality Education for Minorities Report*, Black, poor and non-White students have been largely ignored.

In reality, the socio-economic and educational bifurcation has widened between the nation's urban and suburban school districts. School board members, administrators, teachers, parents, elected officials and the larger public have an ethical, moral and legal responsibility to act in support of educational parity for all of the 40 million children enrolled in over 15,000 autonomous school districts which comprise our national network of public schools.

Today, vis-a-vis, societal challenges, we live in what Charles Dickens once described as *"The best of times, the worst of times."*

Some clear, visceral, compelling, inexorable challenges which must be confronted in a forthright, imaginative, realist and prompt manner if we are to have a nation of equity, wholesome, demonstrable excellence and increased prosperity are as follows:

EQUITABLE FUNDING AND EQUALITY
OF OPPORTUNITY FOR ALL STUDENTS

In some of our suburban school districts, strong and solid property resources and the affluence of the residents enable them to pay three to four times the per capita expendure available to impoverished urban districts. In addition, too many urban school districts are urged *to do more with less.* No such clarion calls are made for such highly affluent school districts as Brooklyn and Newton, Massachusetts, Montgomery County, Maryland, Fairfax, Virginia, Webster Grove, Missouri and Beverly Hills, California. It is totally unfair, illogical and unreasonable to expect that urban and rural school districts will be able to provide high quality education to their educational clientele without requisite human and monetary resources. State governments, which have the legal responsibility for education, must modify funding formulas in order to abate and end current monetary disparities among urban, rural and suburban school districts. The over-arching reason for this effort is that educational excellence is costly.

John Gardner, in his book, *No Easy Victories*, makes a sage point:

> *We cannot have communities half sound and half un¬sound. Bitterness, anger and social disintegration cannot be sealed off. They will inevitably affect the whole community and the whole nation. It isn't going to be a decent society for any of us until it is for all of us. If our sense of responsibility fails us, our sheer self-interest should come to the rescue. (3)*

It is imperative, in our "sheer self-interest" and national interest, to refuse to permit race, class and geography to be the primary determinants of academic excellence and equality of opportunity.

INSIPID, NON-CHALLENGING
AND SUBSTANDARD CURRICULA

It is essential that imaginative, rigorous, systematic and humane curriculum programs be set in place to challenge, stimulate, energize and involve students in substantive and enduring learning episodes. There, too, must be academic-intellectual honesty and integrity in all discrete subject areas which embrace Afrocentric/multicultural and gender diversity, truth, depth and breadth.

Again, John Gardner makes an apt observation:

> *Much education today is monumentally ineffective. All too often, we are giving young people cut flowers when we should be teaching them to grow their own plants. We are stuffing their heads with the products of earlier innovation, rather than teaching them how to innovate. We think of the mind as a storehouse to be filled, rather than as an instrument to be used.*
> *(4)*

The curriculum is the engine of a school district. It has to be well lubricated by administrators and teachers to make certain that the academic potential of students is made kinetic or put into action. Stated differently, the curriculum should provide a framework for a variety of instructional episodes and activities that stretch students' minds to the fullest.

All students, within the framework of a K-12 unified and inclusive curriculum, should have systemic and challenging learning experiences which address the history, problems and accomplishments of disparate ethnic-racial groups. Learning should be directed toward helping students to acquire the higher level cognitive skills of analysis, synthesis and evaluation. Students, too, must be involved in affective skills of valuing, organization and characterization.

In brief, the whole child must be taught in regard to his/her psychomotor, affective and cognitive development.

MAXIMUM INVOLVEMENT OF PARENTS

In order to have safe, orderly, purposeful and productive schools, parents must be involved in a direct and pervasive way. In the past, schools tended to be effective because of a solid, serious and enduring partnership which existed between the school and the home. Today, in too many school districts, a disjunction or abyss exists between schools and parents. This situation needs to be remedied if educational progress is to occur for students. It is patently clear that students tend to achieve at higher levels when schools and parents work in partnership. Schools must make a conscientious, deliberate and assiduous effort to involve parents in the total life of the school community. Enlisting the support of religious institutions, local businesses, civic groups and block clubs will help to facilitate this process. The school and the community must function as one to help students to succeed.

HIGH EXPECTATIONS FOR ALL STUDENTS

All students must be held to the highest academic standards. The problems which confront our public schools are not insoluble. The shining example of Marva Collins with her West Side Preparatory School in Chicago, the dauntless work of James Comer with his "Comer Project" which emphasizes academic and social skills, parental involvement, a strong, vibrant and invigorating curriculum, and the extraordinary work of countless teachers and administrators, Black and White, in our nation's urban centers, are affirmations of hope and stability.

Commitment, persistence and energetic community and fiscal support can enable schools to become serious centers of inquiry and excellence. The fundamental reality is that most youngsters in our schools, public and private, are not being challenged at optimum instructional levels. There is an urgent and critical need to actualize this national potential.

James Comer makes a trenchant observation illustrative of this point in stating that:

> *"By the time they enter school the vast majority of children have the mental equipment required for learning basic skills. What too frequently happens is the relationship of community to school, within-school staff, and teacher-to-child is such that*

too many teachers are not in a position to motivate all children to learn at an optimal level." (5)

Comer concludes in stating:

"Most children who get off to a good start in a school; continue to do well and to acquire the skills necessary to perform well in the society as adults. School is, after all, a template and a reflection of the larger culture." (6)

Demonstrable educational excellence will not take hold and flourish in a school or societal environment of disorder and deviant behavior. The commitment of staff to the "educability of the students, requisite resources, human and monetary, and a summoning and maintaining of will and commitment will permit this process to occur."(7)

All students, too, must be taught that excellence is not Black, White, Yellow, Red, male or female, but universal. Excellence, in fact, is colorless and genderless, but is a universal possibility.

UNRELENTING ADVOCACY FOR PUBLIC SCHOOLS

It falls to all of us to be strong, undeviating, incessant and determined advocates of our nation's public schools, which have developed the most powerful nation in the world. It is we, in a time of enormous tumult, ferment, restive-ness and uncertainty, who must dare to affirm with clarity, strength and power the manifold successes, amidst societal storms, disruptions, austerity and stress of public education. If we believe, in earnest, that our schools can be made better, they will tend to improve. Conversely, if we develop a WOE IS ME MENTALITY ORASACK-CLOTH AND ASHES APPROACH, our public schools will tend to move in the direction of decline, deterioration and neglect.

There is a foot today in our nation a veritable menu of programs which are in various stages of trial or experimentation, such as vouchers, charter schools, privatization, among others, with the aim of ameliorating and sustaining achievement levels. These entities and groups manifest the desirability and need for their educational approaches; the supporters of public education must be visible, direct and forceful in showing, THROUGH DEEDS AND DATA, the continuing strengths, resilience and achievements of public education. This, to be sure, is the season of ACCOUNTABILITY.

In this spirit, education must be a process where the minds of children and youths are challenged and transformed. In addition, the fertile and expansive minds of students, brimming with intellectual curiosity and an irrepressible sense of adventure and wonderment, are liberated and informed to make rational and informed decisions. Education geared to passivity, ennui and docility must be firmly rejected. Analytical and critical thinking, participatory involvement, high self-esteem and risk-taking must suffuse and serve as an educational catalyst for leadership and shared decision-making and not simply fellowship, rote memorization, myth-making and dependency.

Marion Wright Edelman, the sagacious and adroit leader of the Children's Defense Fund, makes a potent and very pertinent point in her engrossing and compelling book, *The Measure of Our Success:*

> *The legacies that parents and church and teachers left of my generation of Black children were priceless but not material: A living faith reflected in daily service, the discipline of hard work and stick-to-it-ness, and a capacity to struggle in the face of adversity. Giving up and "burnout" were not part of the language of my elders—you got up every morning and you did what you had to do and you got up every time you fell down and tried as many times as you had to get it done right. (8)*

Edelman concludes her thought by saying:

> *"I have always believed that I could help change the world because I have been lucky to have adults around me who did— in small and large ways. Most were people of simple grace who understood what Walker Percy wrote: "You can get all A's and still flunk life." (9)*

Just as Marion Wright Edelman and countless others refused let be failure to apart of their lexicons, we must refuse to "flunk" or to further erode public education through our inaction, complacency and apathy. *It is we, as a collective force, who must be in the forefront for the recrudescence, revival and flowering of a precious and incalculable national resource—public education.*

The problems which impinge on our nation's public schools, no matter how vexatious, cumbersome and formidable, are not insoluble. If we utilize our collective talents, abilities and energies, transcending the ancient foes of humanity such as racism, sexism, classism and religious bigotry, we will be able to engender and sustain and educational milieu which will advance the fron¬tiers of learning and excellence in an immeasurable manner. Now is the time to begin a genuine educational renaissance in our nation's public schools for all children and youths.

It will be a costly endeavor. However, as a nation which spends almost one trillion dollars for defense, we can afford to spend more than the present 7 percent of our Gross National Product for education. As a nation which expends over $20,000 for each person incarcerated in our nation's penal institutions, we can afford to fund fully such programs as Head Start, Title I, Aid to Families with Dependent Children, Vocational-Technical education programs, Women, Infant and Children nutritional programs, job training, day care centers, decent, safe, sanitary housing and related programs. What is seriously needed is a national mobilization of will and resources.

We can, as in times past, move forward and upward, if we muster the will to dream and act with the necessary human and monetary resources required to achieve palpable educational excellence. We must dream, I believe, in the spirit of Langston Hughes:

> *"Hold fast to dreams*
> *For if dreams die*
> *Life is a broken-winged bird*
> *That cannot fly."*

I end as I began in affirming the necessity of education as national glue for the world of cybernetics, robotics and the Informative Age. Richard Bach, in his absorbing book, Jonathan Livingston Seagull, describes how Fletcher, a master teacher, teaches the gawky and tremulous Jonathan how to navigate the air waves with grace, confidence and aplomb. Bach concludes the book in a spirit of triumph and joy for Jonathan:

> *And though he tried to look properly severe for his students,*
> *Fletcher Seagull suddenly saw them all as they really were, just*
> *for a moment, and he more than liked he loved what he saw.*
> *No limits, Jonathan? He thought, and he smiled. His race to*
> *learn had begun. (11)*

The time is now at hand to say with passion, authority and an unshakable and unwavering conviction to all children and youths, irrespective of race, gender, ethnicity and socio-economic status, "NO LIMITS." Let us begin this marvelous and essential process congruent with the ancient and time-honored bib¬lical admonition: "VERITAS vo liberatit" (and you shall know the truth, and the truth shall set you free).

Epilogue

I too met Dr. Samuel L. Banks as a beginning social studies teacher. He was a major force, not only in my life, but in the lives of other educators and thousands of children. Each of us is allotted but so many years, so few to spend completing life's tasks. Yet, so few live their lives in service to others. Dr. Banks gave of himself unselfishly. His manner gave us reassurance. His wit and sequipedian vocabulary brightened our days. His sincere and gentle concern for the students and staff of schools, especially those in Baltimore City, gave us the comfort that comes from knowing that another human being cares.

Dr. Banks will be sorely missed, yet he left behind him a powerful legacy of educators and children who expect only the best. He will remain a part of us through fond memories and some of his writings enclosed in this book, so lovingly edited by Collis D. Patterson.

Jacqueline L. Frierson, Ed. D

BIBLIOGRAPHY

<u>Oral Presentation: #1</u>

Allport, Gordon. *The Nature of Prejudice.* Reading, Mass.: Addison-Wesley Publishing Company, 1954.

Banks, Samuel L. *The Education of Black Children and Youths: A Framework for Excellence.* Columbia, MD.: C.F. Fairfax Publishing Com¬pany, 1985.

Clark, Kenneth B. *Prejudice and Your Child.* Boston: Beacon Press, 1963.

Coles, Robert, *Children of Crisis: A Study of Courage and Fear.* Boston: Little, Brown, and Company, 1967.

Comer, James P. *School Power.* New York: The Fire Press in 1980. Maggie's American Dream. New York: New American Library, 1988.

DuBois, William E. B. *The Souls of Black Folk.* Chicago: A. C. McClurg and Company, 1903.

Franklin, John Hope. *From Slavery to Freedom (5th Ed.).* New York: Knopf, 1974.

Harding, Vincent. *There Is A River: The Black Struggle for Freedom In American.* New York: Harcourt Brace, 1981.

Johnson, John. *Succeeding Against the Odds.* New York: Warner Books, 1989.

Jordan, Winthrop. White over Black. Baltimore: Penguin Books, 1968.

Quarles, Benjamin. *The Negro in the Making of America.* New York: Collier, 1964.

Woodson, Carter Godwin. *The Miseducation of the Negro.* Washington, D.C.: Associated Publishers, 1933.

Young, Whitney. *Beyond Racism.* New York: McGraw-Hill Book Co., 1969.

Oral Presentation: #2

Woodson, Carter G. *The Miseducation of the Negro.* Washington, D.C.: The Associated Publishers, p. XIII.

Fishel, Leslie H., Jr. and Quarles, Benjamin. *The Negro American: A Documentary History.* Glenview, IL: Scott, Foresman and Company, 1967, 380 - 381.

Banks, L. Samuel. *The Education of Black Children and Youths: A Framework for Excellence.* Columbia, MD.: C. H. Fairfax Press, 1985, p. 61.-

Oral Presentation: #3

Banks, Samuel L. *Stony the Road: The Black American in the Ameri¬can Experience.* Wheeling, IL. Whitehall Company, 1972, p. 3

Ibid. p. 3.

Franklin, John Hope. *From Slavery to Freedom* (5th Ed.). New York: Alfred A. Knopf, p. 405.

Ibid. p. 406.

Ibid. p. 406.

Ibid. p. 406.

Oral Presentation: #4

Handlin, Oscar. *The Uprooted.* New York: Grosset and Dunlap, 1951, pp. 294 - 295.

Winthrop, Jordan. *White over Black*. Baltimore: Penguin Books, Inc., 1968, p.436.

Franklin, John Hope. *The Militant South*. Cambridge: Belkap Press, 1945, p. 76.

Logan, W. Rayford. *The Negro in the United States: A Brief History*. Princeton: D. Van Nastran Company, Inc., 1957, p. 51.

Fishel, Leslie H., Jr and Quarles, Benjamin. *The Negro American: A documentary History*. Glenview, IL: Scott, Foresmans and Company, 1967, 380 – 381.

Banks, L. Samuel. *The Education of Black Children Youths: A Framework for Excellence*. Columbia, MD.: C.H.Fairfax Press, 1985, p.61. -

Oral Presentation: #5

Williams, Jamye Coleman and Williams, McDonald, Eds. *The Negro Speaks*. New York: Noble and Noble, Publishers, Inc., 1970, p.233

Ibid. pp. 233-234

Jordan, Winthrop D. *White over Black: American Attitudes toward the Negro,* 1550-1812. Baltimore: Penguin Books, Inc., 1968, p. 24.

Ibid. p. 24

Ibid. p. 24

Dubois, William Edward Burghardt: *The Souls of Black Folk*. New York: Signet, 1969, p. 45.

Ibid. p. 45

Robeson, Paul. *Here I Stand*. New York: Beacon Press, 1958, p. 42.

King, Martin Luther, Jr. *Why We Can't Wait*. New York: Signet, 1963, p. 95.

Woodson, Carter Godwin. The Mis-Education of the Negro. Washing¬ton, D.C. Associated Publishers, p. Ill

Ibid. p. III

Ibid. p. III

Banks, Samuel L. Stony the Road: The Black American in the Ameri¬can Experience. Wheeling, IL: Whitehall Press, 1972, p. 81.

Banks, Samuel L. The Education of Black Children and Youths: A Framework for Excellences. Columbia, MD. C. H. Fairfax Company, 1985, p. 63.

Ibid. p. 63.

DuBois. Op. city., p. 139.

Oral Presentation: #7

Schlesinger, Arther, M., Jr. *The Disuniting of America: Reflections on a Multicultural Society.* New York: W.W. Morton and Company, 1991, p. 12.

Ibid. p. 13.

Hacker, Andrew. *Two Nations: Black and White-Separate, Hostile and Unequal.* New York: Charles Scribner's Son, p. 3.

Ibid. p. 219.

Dubois, William Edward Burghardt. *The Autobiography of W.E.B. DuBois*: International Publishers Company, Inc., p. 419.

TRIBUTE TO DR. SAMUEL L. BANKS

You were such a distinguished gentleman and scholar.
You were someone worthy we wanted to follow. Never has such a
honorable role model passed our way.
Dr. Samuel L. Banks, we proudly salute you today.

You were an advocate for all children and human rights.
It did not matter what the color, cause, or fight.
A drum major for justice, we can honestly say.
Dr. Samuel L. Banks, we proudly salute you today.

You were truly a persistent champion for all.
You are still our special hero and you stand very tall.
You can be sure in a remarkable and unique way,
Dr. Samuel L. Banks, we proudly salute you today.

You had a wonderful, gentle, caring attitude, and touch.
To the Baltimore City Public Schools you meant so very much.
You, as a gatekeeper, we certainly could not pay. Dr. Samuel L.
Banks, we proudly salute you today.

You will forever remain foremost in our hearts,
A wonderful blessing never to depart.
A gift lent to us truly from above in every way.
Dr. Samuel L. Banks, we proudly salute you today

Printed with permission

Mary L. Harmon
Baltimore City Public School System